W9-DDR-180

This book is by a man who daily walked and talked with Jesus and had an intimacy with Him in a way few have achieved, but all may achieve.

From the Foreword by
MAX LUCADO

BILL BRIGHT'S
"THE JOY OF KNOWING GOD"
SERIES

the JOY of ACTIVE PRAYER

DR. BILL BRIGHT

The Bible Teacher's Teacher

COOK COMMUNICATIONS MINISTRIES
Colorado Springs, Colorado • Paris, Ontario
KINGSWAY COMMUNICATIONS LTD
Eastbourne, England

Victor® is an imprint of
Cook Communications Ministries,
Colorado Springs, CO 80918
Cook Communications, Paris, Ontario
Kingsway Communications, Eastbourne, England

THE JOY OF ACTIVE PRAYER
© 2005 by Bill Bright

First Printing, 2005
Printed in United States of America
1 2 3 4 5 6 7 8 9 10 Printing/Year 09 08 07 06 05

Cover Design: Brand Navigation, LLC

Library of Congress Cataloging-in-Publication Data

Bright, Bill.
The joy of active prayer : your access to the Almighty / Bill Bright.
    p. cm. -- (The joy of knowing God series ; bk. 6)
    ISBN 0-7814-4251-6 (pbk.)
    1. Prayer. I. Title. II. Series.

BV215.B75 2005
248.3'2--dc22

                                    2004027060

Dedication

GLOBAL FOUNDING PARTNERS

The Bright Media Foundation continues the multifaceted ministries of Bill and Vonette Bright for generations yet unborn. God has touched and inspired the Brights through the ministries of writers through the centuries. Likewise, they wish to pass along God's message in Jesus Christ as they have experienced it, seeking to inspire, train, and transform lives, thereby helping to fulfill the Great Commission each year until our Lord returns.

Many generous friends have prayed and sacrificed to support the Bright Media Foundation's culturally relevant, creative works, in print and electronic forms. The following persons specifically have helped to establish the foundation. These special friends will always be known as Global Founding Partners *of the Bright Media Foundation.*

Bill and Christie Heavener and family

Stuart and Debra Sue Irby and family

Edward E. Haddock Jr., Edye Murphy-Haddock, and the Haddock family

Acknowledgments

It was my privilege to share fifty-four years, six months, and twenty days of married life with a man who loved Jesus passionately and served Him faithfully. Six months before his home going, Bill initiated what has become "The Joy of Knowing God" series. It was his desire to pass along to future generations the insights God had given him that they, too, could discover God's magnificence and live out the wonderful plan He has for their lives.

"The Joy of Knowing God" series is a collection of Bill Bright's top ten life-changing messages. Millions of people around the world have already benefited greatly from these spiritual truths and are now living the exciting Christian adventure that God desires for each of us.

On behalf of Bill, I want to thank the following team that helped research, compile, edit, and wordsmith the manuscripts and audio scripts in this series: Jim Bramlett, Rebecca Cotton, Eric Metaxas, Sheryl Moon, Cecil Price, Michael Richardson, Eric Stanford, and Rob Suggs.

I also want to thank Bill's longtime friends and Campus Crusade associates Bailey Marks and Ted Martin, who carefully reviewed the scripts and manuscripts for accuracy.

Bill was deeply grateful to Bob Angelotti and Don Stillman of Allegiant Marketing Group for their encouragement to produce this series and their ingenuity in facilitating distribution to so many.

A special thanks to Cook Communications and its team of dedicated professionals who partnered with Bright Media Foundation in this venture, as well as to Steve Laube, who brought us together.

Last but not least, I want to express my appreciation to Helmut Teichert, who worked faithfully and diligently in overseeing this team that Bill's vision would be realized, and to John Nill, CEO of Bright Media, who has helped me navigate the many challenges along this journey.

As a result of the hard work of so many, and especially our wonderful Lord's promise of His grace, I trust that multitudes worldwide will experience a greater joy by knowing God and His ways more fully.

With a grateful heart,
MRS. BILL BRIGHT (VONETTE)

Contents

Foreword

The title of this book aptly describes Bill Bright. Connecting the words *joy, active,* and *prayer* together could not be more descriptive of this great man.

Bill was a man of *joy*—the joy of the Lord. He was deeply serious about his mission of helping to fulfill the Great Commission, but he lived it with the pervasive inner joy that comes only from walking in constant fellowship with his Savior, secure in His love and filled with His Spirit. As his friends and associates knew, that inner joy consistently, constantly bubbled outward.

Bill also personified the word *active*. He was a man on the go with mind in gear and body in motion, traveling and speaking city to city, state to state, and nation to nation. Ideas for helping to fulfill the Great Commission exploded in his mind, and his staff raced to keep up. He seemed tireless, even into his late 70s, until sickness finally slowed him, just a little. But even on his sick bed with pulmonary fibrosis and short of breath in his final days, he labored on projects the Lord had given him. This continued until his very last breath. The joy of the Lord was his strength.

Bill Bright was a man of *prayer*, an example to us all. Prayer was the first thing off his lips in the morning and the last thing at night. In between, he conversed with the Lord all day. Bill knew about prayer. Over the years, the Lord showed him many wonderful truths about prayer, and he lived them out.

As you read on, remember this book is by a man who daily walked and talked with Jesus and had an intimacy with Him in a way few have achieved, but all may achieve. That is what this book is all about. Bill deeply desired that you have that same level of intimacy; thus this legacy of his writings.

There was an old television commercial about a financial firm that said, "When EF Hutton speaks, everyone listens." Whenever my dear friend, Bill Bright, spoke, I listened.

I am listening still.

—MAX LUCADO

KEEP ON PRAYING.

1 THESSALONIANS 5:17

—————◆—————

HE DELIGHTS IN THE PRAYERS OF THE UPRIGHT.

PROVERBS 15:8

—————————

1

An Unfathomable Privilege

Have you ever considered that you have immediate access to the most powerful Person in the universe? Over the last fifty-plus years, I have had the honor and privilege of meeting several presidents of the United States. Each one has had a very heavy schedule and tens of thousands of friends and supporters who would have liked to be invited to meet with him. Because of limited time, only a few are invited. Those who are must go through meticulous security checks before they are allowed to meet the president.

As a child of God, you have the opportunity for an instant audience with the King of kings, the Lord of lords, or the President of presidents, if you will. Whatever the need, whatever the time, His calendar is cleared to be with you; His schedule is open for your appointment; His full attention is devoted to you. Do you really believe that? And do you realize what an extraordinary privilege it is? Or do you just take it for granted, without giving it much thought?

I heard of a successful woman named Susie who, because of her superlative experience and skills, was granted a great honor and privilege—she was invited to serve in the office of the president of the United States. The first time she met the president she was awestruck and overwhelmed. She was speechless. She did not know how to communicate and felt frustrated. Many new believers are that way when first talking with God. But the second time she felt a little more at ease. She became more and more at home and found herself coming into the presence of the president with anticipation and excitement. She was no longer reluctant, nor did she continue to feel inadequate.

The more we come into the presence of God, the more comfortable and natural we are around Him.

It is the same in the life of the believer. The more we come into the presence of God, the more comfortable and natural we are around Him. Of course, as Susie was with the president, we, in our relationship with our Lord, are always aware of who He is, and we always behold Him with deep respect and awe. But we are no longer strangers. His presence becomes more of a wonderful and natural experience for us, and yet, in a way, our awe of Him increases too. The more we know Him, the more we adore Him.

And the more we understand who He is and His great grace on our behalf, the more we feel free to come boldly into His presence. The writer of Hebrews exhorts us to "come boldly to the throne of our gracious God. There we will receive his mercy, and we will find grace to help us when we need it" (4:16).

God desires our fellowship and intimacy. That is perhaps the most amazing thing of all: He desires to be with us! The Son of God shed His own blood to provide this access and intimacy. Hebrews 10:20 records, "This is the new, life-giving way that Christ has opened up for us through the sacred curtain, by means of his death for us."

So because of Jesus' work on the cross, we have access to the Creator of the universe. Who can imagine such a thing? But there's even more. Not only do you have the ear of the greatest Person in the universe as you kneel in your place of prayer, but you also have been given the privilege of being used by God to help change the lives of individuals and nations. God has made available to you His vast reservoir of power, wisdom, love, and grace, if only you are willing to believe Him, to trust and obey Him. How can we ever really fathom such a glorious thing?

But Where Is God When I Need Him?

Why is it that God is with us and within us, yet so many of us live with little awareness of His presence? We face life's problems without taking advantage of His wisdom. We cope with crises without calling upon the limitless strength that He has to offer us. Have you made that mistake in your own life? Why does this happen?

You have immediate access to the most powerful Person in the universe.

It certainly is not because God wants it to be so. Psalm 145:18 tells us, "The LORD is close to all who call on him, yes, to all who call on him sincerely." That means the Lord longs to maintain an intimate relationship with every one of us. I believe the key word in that verse is *sincerely*. How sincere are you in calling on the Lord? Do you really want to depend on Him daily? Or are you simply looking for instant help from the immediate problem of the day? Do you wish to partake in a rich and full relationship with the King of all kings? Or are you concerned that He might interfere with the way you want to run your life?

————————❖————————

The more we understand who God is and His great grace on our behalf, the more we feel free to come boldly into His presence.

————————————————

Those impure motives will never cause God to stop reaching out to you, but they will make it much more difficult for you to know the fullness of His love and power. Only when we finally come to a sincere desire for Him, as the psalm indicates, will we discover what He has wanted us to have all along.

The following chapters cover some general and specific aspects on deepening your relationship with God through prayer. Get ready to experience a more intimate prayer life as you interact with Him. You have an unfathomable privilege of knowing and relating with the God of the universe!

2

The Purpose of Prayer

Someone has said, "Prayer is a dialogue between two people who love each other—God and man." To me, real prayer is simply communicating with God, inviting Him to talk to me as I talk to Him. But prayer is much more than words. It is an expression of the heart toward God. It is an experience, a relationship, not an activity.

Because the One to whom you pray is the King of kings and the Lord of lords, the Creator of heaven and earth, you come into His presence with reverence. But He is also your loving heavenly Father who cares for you and delights in having fellowship with you. Therefore, you can enter into His presence with a relaxed, joyful heart, knowing that God loves you more than anyone else has ever loved you or will ever love you.

Every Christian has a direct line of communication with God, available at all times. But most Christians never lift the phone off the hook and often forget the line even exists until an emergency arises.

WHY IS PRAYER IMPORTANT?

For more than a year before Campus Crusade for Christ began, I led church teams into college dormitories, fraternities, and sororities in the Los Angeles area; yet, to my knowledge, not a single person committed his or her life to Christ at any of these meetings.

But when God called this ministry into being in the spring of 1951, we immediately formed a twenty-four-hour prayer chain and divided the prayer time into ninety-six fifteen-minute periods. Scores of Christians invested fifteen minutes in prayer every day on behalf of our new ministry at the University of California in Los Angeles.

During the very first sorority meeting at UCLA after the prayer chain began, more than half of the sixty women present expressed a desire to receive Christ. Over the next few months, more than 250 students at UCLA—including the president of the student body, the editor of the newspaper, and a number of top athletes—committed their lives to Jesus Christ. So great was their influence for Christ that the campus chimes began to play Christian hymns at noon each day!

> *This unprecedented demonstration of God's blessing was no accident. God was responding to the prayers of his children.*

This unprecedented demonstration of God's blessing was no accident. God was responding to the prayers of His children. His blessing continues to this day as He is using Campus Crusade for Christ to help introduce millions of people to our Savior and to build disciples in all the major countries of the world. Prayer continues to be our major emphasis, and God continues to answer.

Because so many Christians—new and old alike—know so little about prayer, I wish to share with you some simple, basic truths and answer some vital questions about prayer.

WHO CAN APPROACH GOD?

Some people believe they are not good enough and not worthy to approach God in prayer. But in addition to you and me, there are more than six billion other imperfect people on planet Earth, all of whom have sinned and fallen short of the glory of God, as Romans 3:23 declares. Who among us dares assume that we can approach the exalted, perfect, holy Creator of the universe, King of kings and Lord of lords?

This unique access to God is provided by the blood of Jesus.

The answer: anyone.

But there is one major prerequisite. In John 14:6, Jesus said, "I am the way, the truth, and the life. No one can come to the Father except through me." Intimate fellowship and communication with God begin when we receive Jesus Christ into our lives as Savior and Lord.

As all Christians should know, this unique access to God is provided by the blood of Jesus, His own perfect and sinless Son, whose death paid the penalty for our sins and opened the way into the Holy of Holies of heaven for all who put their faith in Him. Acts 4:12 says, "There is salvation in no one else! There is no other name in all of heaven for people to call on to save them."

While it is true that we have all sinned and fallen short of

God's glory and that the wages of sin is death, the book of Romans assures us, "but the free gift of God is eternal life through Christ Jesus our Lord" (Romans 6:23). The Lord Jesus Christ, the Son of God, has taken the penalty for all our sins upon Himself. When we receive Him, we become forgiven sinners. And our lines of intimate communication with our heavenly Father are opened again.

THE PRIORITY OF PRAYER

Jesus set the perfect example of obedience in prayer. Although His day was filled from morning to night with many pressures and responsibilities—addressing crowds, healing the sick, granting private interviews, traveling, and training His disciples—He made prayer a top priority. If Jesus was so dependent on this fellowship alone with His Father, how much more should you and I spend time alone with God?

To intercede means to pray for, to plead, to entreat, to stand in the gap for another.

The lives of the disciples and other Christians who have been used mightily of God through the centuries to reach their world for Christ all testify to the necessity of prayer. They, too, are examples of obedience to our Lord's command to pray.

Someone has wisely said, "Satan laughs at our toiling, mocks at our wisdom, but trembles when he sees the weakest saint on his knees." Prayer is God's appointed way of doing God's work.

You can be a prayer intercessor even while confined to a bed or a wheelchair. You can pray anywhere. If you do not have the strength to pray aloud, you can whisper. If you cannot whisper, you can move your lips. If you cannot move your lips, then pray silently, in your mind. God knows and reads your heart.

To *intercede* means to pray for, to plead, to entreat, to stand in the gap for another.

In the Old Testament, the Levitical priest stood between man and God. He represented man to God. But now, Jesus is our High Priest, and the New Testament explains that all believers are priests (see Revelation 1:6). You can exercise your priestly role and stand before God, pleading and interceding for others.

> *As a Spirit-filled follower of Jesus, you are a container of God's power—the same power that raised Christ from the dead.*

Your humble prayers can actually help change your world! You may help touch millions of lives and maybe even help change nations. The apostle Paul said, "When I am weak, then I am strong" (2 Corinthians 12:10).

Are you weak? Then by faith, with Paul, declare that you are strong! God is in you and He is not through with you!

Sometimes God uses His power to anoint talented men and women to raise up huge international ministries that may touch millions or even billions of souls, and we thank God for them. But most times that same power will rest simply on one humble person, a person who in the world's eyes may seem weak, lowly, foolish, and totally without human power and influence. Yet with God's power operating in and through that person, he or she contains all the power of the universe! Such a humble person, without pride and ego, is qualified to receive God's power, actually more than a person self-confident in his or her own abilities. The Bible says, "God deliberately chose things the world considers foolish in order to shame those who think they are wise. And he chose those who are powerless to shame those who are powerful. God chose things despised by the world, things counted as nothing at all, and used them to bring to nothing what the world considers important, so that no one can ever boast in the presence of God" (1 Corinthians 1:27–29).

The people around you may not know it, but you are a spiritual explosion waiting to happen!

As a Spirit-filled follower of Jesus, even in that hospital bed, or in that bed or chair of confinement at home or in a nursing home, you are a container of God's power—the same power that raised Christ from the dead.

"The Spirit of God, who raised Jesus from the dead, lives in you. And just as he raised Christ from the dead, he will give life to your mortal body by this same Spirit living within you" (Romans 8:11).

That power—the Greek word *dunamus*—is where we get the word for *dynamite*. The people around you may not know it, but you are a spiritual explosion waiting to happen!

Like dynamite, God's power is only latent power until it is released. You can release God's dynamite power into people's lives and the world through your faith, your words, and your prayers.

WHY SHOULD WE PRAY?

First, we pray because God commands us to pray. The New Testament commands to pray are many. For example, "Keep on praying" (1 Thessalonians 5:17), or "pray continually"

(NIV). Jesus told His disciples to pray and "never give up" (Luke 18:1).

We also pray because of our Lord's example. Jesus Christ, the very Son of God, was always obedient and diligent in prayer. If He who was perfect prayed, certainly we should.

We pray because of the examples of the disciples and others. The lives of the disciples and the biographies of Christians who have been mightily used of God through the centuries all testify to the absolute necessity of prayer.

To have fellowship with God, we pray. God waits anxiously for you to come to Him in prayer. Proverbs records, "He [the Lord] delights in the prayers of the upright" (15:8). If we wish to please God and to delight Him, time with Him in prayer is a must.

My own sons help me to realize the importance of this fact. No matter how busy I am, when Zachary or Bradley wants to talk with me, I gladly put aside everything else just to have fellowship with either of them. I long and love to be with them, and I am always grateful when they want to be with me.

In a small way, this helps me understand how the great heart of our loving God delights in us and longs for our fellowship.

We pray to communicate with God. He said, "Call to me and I will answer you and tell you great and unsearchable things you do not know" (Jeremiah 33:3 NIV). Prayer is a two-way street. We talk to God, and in turn we hear His voice as He speaks to us.

We also pray to receive spiritual nurture. Just as a child needs food to grow physically, so we need spiritual food to grow spiritually. We can miss a meal and not feel any ill effects, but if we go without food for a week, we begin to weaken and run out of energy. So it is with our spiritual life. Our inner person hungers constantly for communication with God.

As Christians, we pray to become fruitful witnesses for Christ. The divine order is first to talk to God about people and then talk to people about God, sharing who He is with those who don't yet know Him. But witnessing to others is effective only when it is backed up by our prayers—or the prayers of others. I am convinced that the single most important factor in my becoming a Christian was the prayers of my godly mother.

PRAYER CHANGES THINGS

Finally, we pray to obtain results. Genuine, biblically based prayer does change things. Prayer releases God's great power to change the course of nature, people, and nations. The faithful prayers of Spirit-filled, believing Christians have proved this many times over.

Several years ago a terrible brush fire threatened the grounds of Arrowhead Springs (our international headquarters at that time). Many buildings, including the bungalow where Vonette and I lived, came extremely close to being engulfed in flames. Seven of the buildings were destroyed.

After evacuating the grounds, a group of people who remained to fight the fire prayed earnestly at about two-thirty in the afternoon that God would turn the ninety-mile-per-hour winds away from the buildings. We, too, got on our knees and prayed that God would turn the winds.

The heat and smoke became so intense that those who were spraying water on the buildings were forced to lie on the ground in order to breathe. But it just so happened that at about two-thirty, when they were at the point of abandoning our bungalow to the flames that surrounded it on three sides, one of the firefighters observed the flag snapping violently in the wind.

Suddenly, the flag began to turn, and within moments it was flapping in the opposite direction. The winds had shifted and now swept the flames in another direction! They all were awestruck at what God had done before their very eyes.

Yes, prayer truly changes things!

PRAYER IS THE SPARK THAT SETS WORSHIP AFLAME.

3

The Object of Prayer

I f you are a believer, you do not pray to inanimate objects, but to a God who genuinely knows and loves you. Do you sometimes wonder if you should pray to God the Father, the Lord Jesus, or the Holy Spirit?

Because the Father, Son, and Holy Spirit work in perfect unity and harmony, each has a specific role in our prayers. The writer of the book of Hebrews said, "Let us then approach the throne of grace with confidence [boldness], so that we may receive mercy and find grace to help us in our time of need" (4:16 NIV).

But how do we approach the most powerful Presence in the universe? Do we pray directly to Him? Do we pray to Jesus Christ and ask Him to present our needs to the Father? How can we boldly approach such a holy God?

To Whom Do We Pray?

Y ou pray to the Father in the name of the Lord Jesus Christ through the ministry of the Holy Spirit. Jesus said, "When you pray, go into your room, close the door and pray to your

Father, who is unseen. Then your Father, who sees what is done in secret, will reward you" (Matthew 6:6 NIV).

———————❖———————

Your prayers are validated by Jesus Christ and are interpreted to God the Father by the Holy Spirit.

Your prayers are validated by Jesus Christ and are interpreted to God the Father by the Holy Spirit. But since God is one God, manifested in three persons, it is perfectly acceptable to pray to Jesus or to the Holy Spirit. There is no jealousy among the three persons of the Trinity. However, the scriptural pattern that Jesus taught addressed the Father.

HEART TO HEART, SPIRIT TO SPIRIT

We read books on prayer. We try new methods. We wonder if there is some hidden formula or secret that will provide the key to powerful prayer. But in reality there is only one secret, and His name is the Holy Spirit. He carries us beyond our weaknesses and limitations. He carries us directly into the incredible, loving presence of God himself.

Prayer is the most intimate communication ever devised. It is heart-to-heart, spirit-to-Spirit communication between creation and Creator. It is talking with God: asking Him for guidance, praising Him for His goodness, sharing with Him our needs and the needs of others, and knowing by faith that He hears and will grant our requests.

God longs to meet with us in prayer, because prayer represents the difference between truly *knowing* Him and merely knowing *about* Him. You could spend your life studying the works of all the great theologians and read every worthy Christian book ever written about God. You could become an expert on all the facts that have been revealed about Him. But still you would not *know* God—not even remotely—unless you communed with Him in prayer. A six-year-old girl who, with childlike faith, kneels at bedtime could know the Lord more intimately than you do, for even her childish prayer is more intimate and personal than mere theological facts and doctrine. Real, living prayer is crucial, and it is only possible through praying in the Spirit. We'll talk more about praying in the Spirit in the next chapter.

As I live in the Spirit, prayer is the foundation of my day and my way of life. As I awaken each morning, I invite the Lord to work in me and through me. I pray that everything that comes to my mind is filtered through the blood of Christ and the Word of God. And then I turn my thoughts to praise, prayer, and thanksgiving. What an honor to be able to bring our concerns to the One who made us and holds the universe together. As long as we can pray, there is hope in all things. If a family member is lost without Christ, prayer can make the difference. If a boss is overwhelming us with work, we have a place to take our concerns. If we are disappointed and heartbroken over a struggling marriage, we need never give up. We know there is always prayer.

> *God longs to meet with us in prayer, because prayer represents the difference between truly knowing Him and merely knowing about Him.*

Cherish this verse in your heart: "The effective prayer of a righteous man can accomplish much" (James 5:16 NASB).

HOW THE HOLY SPIRIT HELPS US PRAY

In the days when the temple was still in use in Jerusalem, only the high priest was allowed to enter the Holy of Holies to atone for the sins of the people—and this only once a year. When he entered that sacred place, he came into the very presence of God. An individual's closest

encounter with God would be to interact with the priest on the public side of the curtain.

As long as we can pray, there is hope in all things.

Yet, as believers, now we can go past the curtain. We can approach the eternal, infinite Creator God of the universe any time of the day, any day of the year. Why? Because of the selfless sacrifice of our Savior Jesus. We can now "boldly enter heaven's Most Holy Place" (Hebrews 10:19).

The Spirit is the One who eagerly clasps your hand and walks you into God's throne room. "Now all of us, both Jews and Gentiles, may come to the Father through the same Holy Spirit because of what Christ has done for us" (Ephesians 2:18).

We should look upon prayer as the most precious, valuable privilege we could ever receive. We should take advantage of it at every available instant and with eagerness: "So let us come boldly to the throne of our gracious God. There we will receive his mercy, and we will find grace to help us when we need it" (Hebrews 4:16).

The Spirit does a number of wonderful things to help us in our prayer life.

THE HOLY SPIRIT PROMPTS US TO PRAY

Have you ever felt that little nudge? You may be going about your business, your mind on many earthly matters, when you sense a little mental tug. You feel the urge to pray about a particular matter or person. This impression could even wake you in the middle of the night. We hear of many Christians who, in various situations, were led to pray for a loved one or friend, only to find that this person was in a dangerous situation at that very moment.

Some time ago I felt a strong impression to pray for an outstanding man the Lord

> *"The effective prayer of a righteous man can accomplish much"* *(James 5:16).*

has used to impact 120 countries. I prayed for him only to feel yet another prompting, an urge to call my friend. So I dialed his telephone number. When I asked my friend how he was doing, he told me that it was the worst day of his life. He began to describe in detail the awful things that were happening to him that day. I tried to minister to his needs, sharing some similar experiences from my own life and how God had worked in the midst of them. Finally we prayed together.

At the end of the conversation, I could tell my friend had new strength and encouragement. He was amazed that I had called him at the very moment he needed encouragement. The Holy Spirit had used me to bring him comfort. I was glad that I had paid attention when the Holy Spirit had prompted me to pray for my friend. This has been my experience on numerous occasions.

THE HOLY SPIRIT GUIDES OUR PRAYERS

The Holy Spirit also molds and shapes our prayers, helping them to be effective and consistent with the will of God. He guides us through the needs of the day, through the emotions of the hour, and through recollections of people we care about. He helps us pray for all the many things we need to bring before the Father.

As He does this, something wonderful happens. The Spirit brings our desires into conformity with God's will. It may be that you have encountered a very difficult situation in life. You feel a great deal of anxiety, and naturally you ask God for a change in the circumstances. But as the days and prayers move by, you find that the circumstances remain the same while your attitude has utterly changed. You suddenly comprehend how God could use someone like you in just such a setting. You realize that He didn't want to help you out of this mess, but to help you through it. More miracles happen in the midst of a crisis than when we are fleeing from our circumstances.

The Holy Spirit helps us pray beyond our many limitations.

God's Spirit guides your prayer over time, until you are asking for Him to lead you rather than remove you from a given situation. The Bible assures us, "God is working in you, giving you the desire to obey him and the power to do what pleases him" (Philippians 2:13).

You pray for God to change things, but in the process, you are the one changed. When you feel the pull of the Spirit to turn your heart toward prayer, you can be joyful in realizing that you will be even closer to the wonderful purposes of God by the time you have finished. The Spirit guides our prayer, and best of all He guides our spirits toward God.

THE HOLY SPIRIT INTERCEDES FOR US IN PRAYER

Here is one of the most remarkable promises and supernatural ministries of the Spirit in prayer. "In the same way, the Spirit helps us in our weakness. We do not know what we ought to pray for, but the Spirit himself intercedes for us with groans that words cannot express" (Romans 8:26 NIV). I have always found this to be a

You pray for God to change things, but in the process, you are the one changed.

tremendously encouraging concept. You may say, "But I don't know how to pray!" Every believer should learn to pray biblically, but that is not the major issue. The Spirit prays for those things we lack the understanding to pray for. He also expresses the depth of emotion that we might feel if we could see with complete spiritual clarity. He helps us pray beyond our many limitations. Knowing this makes me all the more eager to pray, as I am sure it does you.

The Holy Spirit knows us better than we know ourselves. He understands our desires, our fears, our strengths, and our weaknesses. He knows what we need before we even know to ask for it. The Holy Spirit, the third person of the Trinity, knows the mind of God. "He who searches our hearts knows the mind of the Spirit, because the Spirit intercedes for the saints in accordance with God's will" (Romans 8:27 NIV). Who better to speak to our heavenly Father for us than the Holy Spirit?

We have so many limitations, so many failings. But we can be joyful in the realization that the Spirit of God stands in the gap, interceding for us. Your prayers are more powerful than you can possibly realize, because He enhances and enlarges them.

THE HOLY SPIRIT LEADS US IN PRAYERFUL WORSHIP

Prayer, of course, is more than a flood of requests. The Spirit helps us to praise and exalt God when we pray. He gives us the realization of the awesomeness of God. He leads us to comprehend just how infinite, how majestic, and how sovereign He truly is, and then, as a result, we can do nothing other than worship in spirit and in truth.

The Spirit leads us to comprehend just how infinite, how majestic, and how sovereign He truly is.

The Spirit frees us from the monotony and dryness of dead prayer by filling our hearts with the wonderful music of true worship. Music begins where words leave off, and sometimes the only way to express our feelings about God's greatness is through the transcendence of melody and verse. Paul urged us, "Let the Holy Spirit fill and control you. Then you will sing psalms and hymns and spiritual songs among yourselves, making music to the Lord in your hearts" (Ephesians 5:18–19). The Spirit makes worship a natural and joyful thing, not merely at church but wherever we may be.

You will find that prayer is the spark that sets worship aflame. You may begin a devotional time with a mood nowhere close to that of worship. But then, as you praise your Lord for His many benefits, as you thank Him for all He has done in your life, as you realize all the many requests you are allowed to bring before Him—what can you do but exalt and magnify His name? You will break out in song within your heart, for words will not be enough. Then you will feel mentally, emotionally, and spiritually refreshed for having worshiped. The Spirit, in His wisdom, knew you needed that. So He became your worship leader.

In each of these ways, the Spirit makes the difference in our prayer. The next chapter reveals how to "pray in the Spirit" along with the power of prayer.

---❖---

GOD WILL HEAR YOUR PRAYER—AND ANSWER—
ACCORDING TO HIS OWN PLANS AND DIVINE TIMING.

4

The Power of Prayer

We have seen some of the many ministries of the Holy Spirit in prayer. But how can we be caught up in the kind of prayer that allows us to sense the transforming presence of God? There are a number of considerations to remember.

We need to avoid certain common misunderstandings. Too often we feel that God is impressed by our verbal eloquence or the length of our prayers. He has no particular regard for either of these. A prayer from the heart, whatever the eloquence or length, is what He looks for. He wants us to pray in the very midst of our life and emotions. These are the times when we are likely to lift up the most heartfelt prayers.

PRAY IN THE SPIRIT

Paul wrote, "Pray in the Spirit on all occasions with all kinds of prayers and requests" (Ephesians 6:18 NIV). Your most effective prayers may come in the most unlikely places—though we never become so "informal" that we lose sight of the greatness and awesomeness of the One to whom we are praying. This brings us to our first suggestion for "praying in the Spirit," which simply means to pray as the Holy Spirit directs you.

ADDRESS GOD RESPECTFULLY

To pray in the Spirit is to pray with a reverent heart. We should never come before God without reverence and awe. "Since we are receiving a kingdom that cannot be destroyed, let us be thankful and please God by worshiping him with holy fear and awe" (Hebrews 12:28). *Fear* is a word that is often missing today from our understanding of a relationship with God, but I believe it refers to a surpassing sense of how awesome and holy God is. When we come to grips with these realities, we are humbled, and God rewards the humble. The prophet Isaiah proclaimed, "The high and lofty one who inhabits eternity, the Holy One, says this: 'I live in that high and holy place with those whose spirits are contrite and humble. I refresh the humble and give new courage to those with repentant hearts'" (Isaiah 57:15).

We also feel joyfully thankful when we pray as the Holy Spirit leads. Do you spend as much time expressing gratitude as you do asking for more blessings? If not, this is a sign that you are not truly praying in the Spirit, who will usher you into God's presence and fill you with a thankful heart. You should have times of prayer that are completely given to thanking Him. The next time you cannot feel the presence of God, and you struggle to find an attitude of worship, spend some time expressing your gratitude. You will be amazed at how quickly your mood will change.

> *To pray in the Spirit is to pray with a reverent heart.*

INITIATE TRANSPARENT CONVERSATION WITH GOD

Praying as the Spirit leads also gives us the freedom to be ourselves. As we have seen in James 5:16 (NASB), "the effective prayer of a *righteous* man can accomplish much." If we have confessed our sin, we realize there is no obstacle between God and us. We can be completely open and honest, telling Him exactly what is on our hearts. "If our conscience is clear, we can come to God with bold confidence. And we will receive whatever we request because we obey him and do the things that please him" (1 John 3:21–22). The key to answered prayer, then, is being in harmony with God. As we come into His presence and know Him more fully, that harmony occurs.

No relationship can be deep and strong without honest communication, and your relationship with God is no different. We experience wonderful liberation when we learn what it is like to be completely honest with God, with no shame or striving to be something we are not. We can worship Him "in spirit and in truth," as Jesus told the woman at the well (John 4:23). When you pray in the Spirit, you will be transparent with God. He knows all that is inside us anyway.

Speak to God as your Father, your dearest Friend. Speak simply and honestly with Him, telling Him the deepest concerns and emotions you are feeling. Open up with full transparency.

DECLARE YOUR CONFIDENCE IN GOD

There is no need to come before God with hesitation and timidity, as if we lack trust in His power. We are praying to the Creator and Sustainer of the universe. If we are praying as the Spirit directs, we can confidently come before Him with our requests.

This means fully realizing our dependence upon Him. One of the most essential effects of prayer is the way it reminds us how helpless we are apart from Him. Each day we must submit ourselves to His lordship again, because our spirits are rebellious and stubborn. As we come before God, we acknowledge our limitations. We cast ourselves upon His mercy and His power, affirming that we can do no good thing on our own.

We do not serve a God of convenience but a God of perfect timing.

Then, having felt our own helplessness, we express faith in His worthiness. Praying as the Spirit directs strengthens our understanding that though we are weak, God is strong. As we pray, we *believe*—we believe that He will act as He desires. We believe He will work through us. We believe that He is totally sovereign. Faith is strengthened when we pray in the Spirit, and we begin to live in the confident assurance that He is Lord and that He is working in our world and through us. Praying in the power of the Holy Spirit always leads to greater confidence and hope in God.

In the matter of prayer, perseverance counts. Faith that God will act is not the same as faith that God will act today, tomorrow, or whatever my schedule may be. He wants us to pray without ceasing, to keep praying with persistence. He knows that the discipline of sustained prayer is good for us. We do not serve a God of convenience but a God of perfect timing—a timing we usually will not know in advance. Keep on keeping on as you pray in the Spirit with faith and endurance. Never give up!

God gave me a vision in 1945 to produce a film on the life of Jesus. The vision became a reality thirty-three years later.

God gave me a vision to train world leaders. Twenty-five years later, that vision became a reality. Always keep on believing; God's timing is perfect.

HOW PRAYER REVEALS HIS POWER

I believe the greatest revelation of God's power in the world comes through the vehicle of our prayers, as guided by the Holy Spirit. Prayer, often with fasting, accomplishes what nothing else will. It softens hearts. It calls friends and enemies to repentance. It reaches far beyond the borders of our mundane life to the other side of the globe and to generations yet unborn. It demolishes the Devil's strongholds. Most important of all, it draws us into intimate communion with our awesome God. God is manifest in His magnificent glory through the prayers of His children. (See appendix E for basic steps to take for successful prayer and fasting.)

There are so many true stories that illustrate the glorification of God and His power through the prayers of faithful believers that an entire library would be needed to contain them. Let me share one example.

In the mid-1800s, the great explorer David Livingstone feared for his life. As the sun set on his small camp in the interior of Africa, he knew the local tribe planned to attack that night and kill him and all of those by his side. Even in the midst of these warnings, Livingstone was strangely filled with peace: God was with him, and God could always be trusted. That night, Livingstone slept without anxiety—and his camp was unthreatened.

Two years later, a miracle happened: The chief of that hostile tribe became a Christian. Livingstone was eager to learn the story of why the tribe had never attacked on that memorable evening. The chief confirmed to him that an uprising had indeed been planned. They had left their settlement with weapons, anger, and the intent to kill. But as the warriors approached Livingstone's camp, they had been surprised by what they saw: Forty-seven mighty warriors guarding the place where the famous explorer slept.

Livingstone was shocked to hear this because he knew there had been no guards. What was the truth?

On a visit home to England, he found out. Livingstone was informed that on that night of crisis two years earlier, across the ocean in Scotland, forty-seven church members had gathered, drawn by the Spirit, to pray fervently for Livingstone. Those prayer warriors stood watch over Livingstone before Almighty God, and his life was spared.

When people are caught up in the Spirit to pray before God, incredible things happen all around us. We release His miraculous power to a world that has forgotten how powerful God is. Forty-seven believers, deep in prayer, were enough to turn back a murderous attack. What would happen in this world if all of God's children became prayer warriors, available to the call of the Spirit to lift up His name and His purposes? How would your life change if you began to pray in the manner described in this chapter?

EXTRAORDINARY ANSWERS TO PRAYER

Let me give you another example of the extraordinary power of prayer.

It was 1947. I was only a young man at the time. But God put it on my heart to pray for the Soviet Union. I don't know why. I had never been there. But in His wisdom and sovereignty, it was just something the Lord put on my heart. I started praying for the Soviet Union that year, and I prayed for years and then for decades, without ever seeing any results.

In the 1980s things looked worse than ever, because after several ineffectual leaders, the Soviet Union was led by President Mikhail Gorbachev, who was at that time riding a tremendous crest of popularity and great power. But President Gorbachev was only a man, and the Bible says, "The Lord directs the king's thoughts. He turns them wherever he wants to" (Proverbs 21:1 TLB).

Our Russian representative living in the Soviet Union at the time was teaching in a very prestigious school for the children of ambassadors from various countries. He told my wife, Vonette, and me that we should organize a twenty-four-hour, thirty-day prayer vigil and encourage Christians all over the world to pray for the liberation of the Soviet Union. Vonette was then chairman of the International Lausanne Intercessory Prayer Committee, a Billy Graham ministry to millions. In response to our representative's prompting, she sent out a plea to Christian leaders representing many millions of people all over the world, asking them to pray that God would do something dramatic to liberate the people of the Soviet empire during that thirty-day period.

Russia had previously known 900 years of Christianity, but for the preceding seventy years or so had been under the oppressive, anti-God communists. We felt strongly led by the Holy Spirit that we should pray that the people of the Soviet Union would be liberated out of their bondage.

Then, with incredible timing, we saw one of the most

Then, with incredible timing, we saw one of the most dramatic answers to prayer that I have ever observed.

dramatic answers to prayer that I have ever observed. The thirty days passed, and, miracle of miracles, the very first working day following those thirty days, President Gorbachev announced new freedoms through what was called *glasnost* (openness) and *perestroika* (restructuring). That was the beginning of the end of the Soviet Union and the beginning of religious freedom to a nation of nearly 300 million people at that time. The rest, of course, is history. Through Campus Crusade and many other ministries there has since been an explosion of the gospel in Russia and other countries of the former Soviet Union.

> *Prayer influences men and nations in accordance with God's promises and purposes.*

Thousands of people prayed, but it could have been the added prayer of a single, little, weak, humble prayer warrior that turned the tide and made the difference. God often orchestrates prayer, involving many people. But if one person had failed to pray, possibly some infirm senior citizen, the results may not have been the same. There is no doubt that prayer influences men and nations in accordance with God's promises and purposes.

Ask the Holy Spirit to give you a similar burden and leading for our country or another nation or group of people. Maybe it will be China, South Asia, Africa, Europe, North America, South America, or some other country or area. When He does, obediently step out in faith with that God-given burden, pray, ask and keep on asking, and believe God's promises.

God will hear—and answer—according to His own

plans and divine timing. And you will be an important part of that plan.

WHEN SHOULD WE PRAY?

Tremendous answers to prayer make one wonder if there is a best time to pray. When should we pray? There is a sense in which I pray continually, talking to God hundreds of times a day about everything. But there are also specific times that I set aside, and these are vital in the believer's prayer life. I begin my day on my knees in prayer, worshiping, praising, and adoring our great and gracious Creator, God, and Father.

Since my last conscious thoughts are of Him, my subconscious thoughts will continue to worship Him all night long.

I acknowledge Jesus Christ as my Lord and Master. By faith, as an act of my will, I appropriate the fullness of the Holy Spirit. I pray for wisdom about the numerous decisions I must make that day. I pray for the salvation of friends and strangers, the healing of the sick, and the spiritual and material needs of the Campus Crusade for Christ ministry, as well as the needs of various staff members and leaders of other Christian organizations and their ministries. I pray for our leaders and for those in authority over us. I even pray about small personal matters that are of concern to me alone. And God answers!

I then like to spend whatever time is appropriate reading and meditating on God's Word. I often kneel quietly before the open Bible and talk with God. I ask the Holy Spirit, who inspired its writings, to make my reading meaningful and edifying to me.

As I read, I pause to thank God for His loving salvation

and provision, to confess any sins in my life that the Scriptures may reveal, to ask Him for the boldness and faith His apostles displayed, and to thank Him for new insights into His divine strategy for reaching the world with the good news of His love and forgiveness through Jesus Christ our Lord. I often pause to pray about some special truth or claim a promise.

Then again, at the end of the day I kneel once again to worship my Lord, to read His Word, and to ask of Him, "Lord, is there anything in me that is displeasing to You, anything I need to confess?" If the Holy Spirit reveals any sins and weaknesses, I confess them and claim by faith God's victory for my life. Then I can know that since my last conscious thoughts are of Him, my subconscious thoughts will continue to worship Him all night long. Thus when I awaken again, my first thoughts will be of our dear Lord.

5

Praying with Confidence

Obedient followers of God desire to glorify Him with their lives. Yet there are times when our prayers seem ineffective. What hinders our prayer? If it is faith in Christ and receiving Him into our hearts that provides the open door, once inside the door, then what? How do we make our intercessions pleasing to God and successful? The fact is that every believer has access to God, but only those who walk in faith and obedience to Christ can expect to receive answers to their prayers.

That's because praying with a clean heart is vital. The psalmist said, "If I had not confessed the sin in my heart, my Lord would not have listened" (Psalm 66:18). We cannot realistically expect God to answer our prayers if there is unconfessed sin in our life. That unconfessed sin blocks our relationship with Him, because He is a holy God.

One of the most frequent hindrances to prayer is an unforgiving spirit. In the Gospel of Mark, chapter 11, Jesus said, "When you are praying, first forgive anyone you are holding a grudge against, so that your Father in heaven will forgive your sins, too" (v. 25). We must come to God with a forgiving heart if we are to receive the believer's legacy of power in prayer.

In addition, we must have a *believing* heart if we expect God to answer our prayers. In Matthew, Jesus said, "If you believe, you will receive whatever you ask for in prayer" (21:22), and "Because of your faith, it will happen" (9:29). These promises are qualified. We must obey and we must trust God.

> *If you know you are abiding in Christ, are controlled by the Holy Spirit, and are praying according to the Word and will of God, you can absolutely expect God to answer your prayer.*

Jesus promised, "If you stay joined to me and my words remain in you, you may ask any request you like, and it will be granted!" (John 15:7). Yet few of us take these words seriously, and few dare to claim what God has so generously promised us.

Let us be obedient, praying, and believing people. The world is waiting to be reached for Christ, and Christ is waiting for us to pray.

EXPECTATION OF SUCCESS

Four words can help us pray with confidence and an expectation of success: *abide, ask, believe*, and *receive*.

ABIDE

First of all, Jesus said that abiding is the key to successful praying. "If you abide in Me, and My words abide in you, ask whatever you wish, and it will be done for you" (John 15:7 NASB). In other words, if you are abiding in Christ—if your life is totally yielded to Him and His Word is abiding in you so that you know His will—you can ask anything you want because your will is to do His will. Abiding, then, is living a life of faith and obedience in the fullness of the Holy Spirit, surrendered to the lordship of Christ with no unconfessed sin, and being totally available to God.

ASK

Second, if we expect answers to our prayers, we must ask. James wrote, "You do not have because you do not ask. You ask and do not receive, because you ask with wrong motives, so that you may spend it on your pleasures" (James 4:2–3 NASB). Jesus said, "If you ask Me anything in My name, I will do it…. Until now you have asked for nothing in My name; ask, and you will receive, that your joy may be made full" (John 14:14; 16:24 NASB).

Abiding is living a life of faith and obedience in the fullness of the Holy Spirit, surrendered to the lordship of Christ with no unconfessed sin, and being totally available to God.

In His Sermon on the Mount, Jesus said, "Ask, and it will be given to you; seek, and you will find; knock, and it will be opened to you. For everyone who asks receives, and he who seeks finds, and to him who knocks it will be opened" (Matthew 7:7–8 NASB).

The unsolved problems in the world are so great that they are almost without number. People are still sick, souls are yet unreached for Christ, evil people still wield ungodly political and financial power, and many injustices continue—largely because the children of God do not ask!

BELIEVE

Third, Jesus promised in Matthew 21:22 (NASB), "And all things you ask in prayer, believing, you will receive." Believing is at the heart of answered prayer. But how do you get this faith to believe? Should you try to work up some kind of state of mind that will in some way equal faith? Of course not.

God does not require you to have great faith. You simply are to have faith in a great God. Jesus said, "Truly I say to you, if you have faith the size of a mustard seed, you will say to this mountain, 'Move from here to there,' and it will

> ❖
>
> *God does not require you to have great faith. You simply are to have faith in a great God.*

move; and nothing will be impossible to you" (Matthew 17:20 NASB).

James instructed us to "ask in faith without any doubting, for the one who doubts is like the surf of the sea, driven and tossed by the wind. For that man ought not to expect that he will receive anything from the Lord, being a double-minded man, unstable in all his ways" (James 1:6–8 NASB).

You see, it's the quality, not the quantity, of the faith that is important.

Faith comes from God (Ephesians 2:8–9). It is not something you try to muster on your own. A life of faith is experienced only by those who walk in obedience. You cannot be on the throne of your life and still pray in faith. You will never meet a person who has great faith in a great God who refuses to obey the God in whom he is commanded to place his trust.

After we believe, we must receive, but before I discuss

receiving, let me say a few more things about faith and believing, because the importance of faith cannot be overstressed.

The Holy Spirit uses three basic means to produce belief in the one praying.

1. *He uses the Word of God.* As you study the Scriptures, you learn more and more about the character of God—His love, His wisdom, His power, His works, His sovereignty, His promises. The more you know of God, the more you trust Him. Paul wrote, "So faith comes from hearing, and hearing by the word of Christ" (Romans 10:17 NASB).

2. *He uses fellowship with other Christians and various circumstances and experiences.* For example, your faith in God grows as you observe a friend being used of God to introduce others to Christ. When he shares his experience with you, this encourages you to believe that God can use you, too.

Imagine right now that you are receiving the answer to your request, and begin to thank God for it.

3. *He uses strong impressions or convictions.* Paul wrote in Philippians 2:13, "For God is working in you, giving you the desire to obey him and the power to do what pleases him." For example, five high school students began to sense their responsibility to God according to Matthew 28:18–20 to share Him with others. Each of these students felt impressed to make a list of three friends whom he wanted to claim for Christ. The first week they met daily to pray that these friends would sense their need of God. The second week they prayed to be instruments of God. The third week they prayed for opportunities to speak to their

friends about Christ. That week fifteen students received the Savior.

RECEIVE

Fourth, we must receive God's answers to our prayers. Receiving means claiming the answer to your request by faith. If you know you are abiding in Christ, are controlled by the Holy Spirit, and are praying according to the Word and will of God, you can absolutely expect God to answer your prayer (see 1 John 5:14–15). So be prepared to receive the answer. Imagine right now that you are receiving the answer to your request, and begin to thank God for it.

> *It is a simple fact that whatever you vividly imagine, ardently desire, sincerely believe, and enthusiastically act upon must inevitably come to pass—assuming, of course, that there is scriptural authority for it.*

In 1954, Roger Bannister broke the four-minute mile. It had never been broken in all the centuries of recorded history, but Bannister believed it could be done. He developed a mental picture of himself breaking the four-minute barrier, and he did it. Since 1954, several hundred other athletes have broken the four-minute mile, simply because Roger Bannister proved that it could be done.

If an individual with only human resources is able to accomplish outstanding success, how much more can you accomplish when you place your faith in the omnipotent God and draw upon His supernatural, inexhaustible resources?

It is a simple fact that whatever you vividly imagine, ardently desire, sincerely believe, and enthusiastically act upon must inevitably come to pass—assuming, of course, that there is scriptural authority for it.

GOD'S PROMISES ABOUT PRAYER

It is estimated that there are more than 5,000 personal promises in the Bible. However, these promises mean little or nothing to many Christians because they do not claim them by faith (see Hebrews 4:2).

Faith is a word signifying action. For example, bags of cement sitting in a warehouse will never become concrete until they are mixed with sand, gravel, and water. Likewise, God's promises will never become concrete unless they are mixed with faith and action. You must make them yours by believing them and putting your faith to work. Which of God's promises do you need most to apply to your own prayer life right now? (See appendix A: God's Promises and Prevailing Prayer.)

PREVAILING PRAYER

Intercessory prayer (praying for the needs of others), offered in a righteous spirit, can actually influence the course of history. It has happened many times in

Every believer has access to God, but only those who walk in faith and obedience to Christ can expect to receive answers to their prayers.

the past; in fact I believe it happens every day. In 1934, just to cite one example, a farmer asked a group of his friends to come to his farm and spend the day in prayer. He was just an ordinary farmer. As the men prayed together, they felt compelled to ask God to raise up a man from their city to carry the gospel to the ends of the earth. There was no immediate answer. But the farmer's teenage son became a believer during an evangelistic crusade that year. Although you would not recognize the farmer's name, you most likely have heard of his son: my friend Billy Graham.

That farmer was a world shaker, because God answered his simple prayer. Never forget that you have every opportunity that farmer had.

During his lifetime, George Müeller recorded more than 50,000 answers to prayer. He prayed for two men daily for more than sixty years. One of these men was converted shortly before Müeller's death and the other about a year later. As in Müeller's experience, we do not always see the answers to our prayers right away. However, we must persevere and leave the results to God.

One of the great needs of today is for men and women who will begin to pray boldly, according to God's will and promises, and, by faith, pray repeatedly and consistently until God moves the mountains in their lives so He is glorified and His purposes are accomplished.

6

Believing God for the Great Commission

Reaching the world for Christ remains high on God's agenda. This objective should be high on the Christian's priority list too.

Consider, again, the Great Commission. For many years since the memorable moment when God gave me the vision for the ministry of Campus Crusade for Christ, I have been strongly impressed that the Holy Spirit wants the Great Commission fulfilled in our generation. Since that original deep impression in 1951, the Great Commission has been my number-one priority as an expression of my love for our Lord and my desire to obey Him.

I have a vivid mental picture of what fulfilling the Great Commission will involve: saturating a world of more than six billion people with the message that Jesus Christ is "the way, the truth, and the life" (John 14:6); discipling tens of millions; training key leader representatives in each of the hundreds of nations and protectorates of the world; and using every modern means of technology—radio, television, high-speed presses, audiovisuals in all forms, satellites, and air travel—to communicate God's love worldwide.

We have had an ongoing strategy for accomplishing this goal, and Christians from more than 196 nations around the world are a part of it. Millions of believers within thousands of churches, denominations, organizations, and mission agencies are uniting to make fulfilling the Great Commission a priority for their evangelism and discipleship ministries at home and abroad.

I sincerely believe that the Great Commission will be fulfilled because it is God's idea, not man's.

I see clearly with my mind's eye a day in the immediate future when billions of people on earth will become aware of the great truths concerning God's love and forgiveness in Jesus Christ and will crown Him Lord of lords. I know that the fulfillment of the Great Commission is the will of God because it is His command and the desire of His heart, and I ardently long to have it come to pass.

Furthermore, I sincerely believe that the Great Commission will be fulfilled because it is God's idea, not man's. It is inconceivable to me that our Lord would have given us the command without giving us the needed resources with which to fulfill His command.

And finally, because I so vividly imagine, ardently desire, and sincerely believe in the fulfillment of the Great Commission in my generation, I can enthusiastically act upon my belief by giving myself completely to the task and helping to mobilize millions of others toward its fulfillment.

THE GREAT COMMISSION AND YOU

Let me encourage you to determine, on a clearly scriptural basis, what God would have you vividly imagine, ardently desire, sincerely believe, and enthusiastically act upon to help fulfill the Great Commission in your home, community, state, nation, and world.

You can tap the Source of power. It may be that, in addition to your own personal ministry, God would have you pray for the personnel of a radio or television station or the staff of a newspaper to be an influence for righteousness. It may be that He would have you claim for Him a high school or college campus, or your workplace; or that every person within a one-mile radius of your home—or every home in the entire city—would be personally visited by trained persons who would lovingly, prayerfully, and intelligently present the claims of Christ.

Remember that as you bow in prayer, you are tapping a source of power that can change the course of history. God's mighty power, His love, His wisdom, and His grace are available to you if you will but believe Him and claim them. Remember always, Jesus promised that you would do the same miracles He did, and even greater ones (see John 14:12).

Will you join with us in praying for the Lord of the harvest to send forth millions of disciples to work with thousands of local churches of all denominations and with various Christian movements and organizations that desire to see the Great Commission fulfilled in this generation?

Will you pray also for a mighty outpouring of God's Holy Spirit upon the entire world and for the funds and materials needed to fulfill this God-given task?

Prayer is the greatest privilege of the Christian life and the most revolutionary source of power known to humanity. If you were to take seriously the promises of God and begin to claim by faith in prayer all that you have been promised, you would experience miracles in your life and ministry, multitudes would be introduced to our Lord Jesus Christ, the whole course of history would be changed, and you would help to fulfill the glorious Great Commission.

HELP OUR UNBELIEF!

Why are we so spiritually impotent and fruitless today compared to the first-century Christians? I believe the answer is *unbelief.*

Our Lord Jesus Christ has commissioned us, as a demonstration of His loving concern and compassion for the world, to go and share the good news of the gospel everywhere. But we huddle in unbelief in our little prayer meetings and talk of peripheral, superficial matters. We are content to see accomplished in the name of Christ only what we are capable of accomplishing through our own intellect, eloquence, and organizational skills. Instead of calling upon the mighty God of the universe and believing Him for the supernatural, we go aimlessly on our way— spiritually impotent, unbelieving, and fruitless.

FIRST-CENTURY POWER

The disciples knew and prayed to the omnipotent Creator God. In response to their prayers and dedicated lives, He used them as ambassadors for Christ to turn a wicked Roman Empire upside down. Read their prayer as recorded in Acts:

"O Lord, Creator of heaven and earth and of the sea and everything in them—you spoke long ago by the Holy Spirit through our ancestor King David, your servant, saying, 'Why do the heathen rage against the Lord, and the foolish nations plan their little plots against Almighty God? The kings of the earth unite to fight against him, and against the anointed Son of God!'

"That is what is happening here in this city today! For Herod the king, and Pontius Pilate the governor, and all the Romans—as well as the people of Israel—are united against Jesus, your anointed Son, your holy servant. They won't stop at anything that you in your wise power will let them do. And now, O Lord, hear their threats, and grant to your servants great boldness in their preaching, and send your healing power, and may miracles and wonders be done by the name of your holy servant Jesus."

ACTS 4:24–30 TLB

Is it any wonder that God used these first-century Christians to change the course of history? They knew and served the mighty, sovereign, loving God of the universe. The God whom you worship and serve is the same all-wise, all-powerful, loving God and Father whom they loved and served. His power has not changed—He longs to do the same through you and me that He accomplished through those first-century believers.

—❖—

Communing with God is the ultimate adventure, and it is available today, tomorrow, and every moment you live.

STRATEGIC PRAYER MOVEMENTS

I believe it is time for Christians to mobilize in prayer and put an end to a dead, dry prayer life. Communing with God is the ultimate adventure, and it is available today, tomorrow, and every moment you live on this planet. I have seen the amazing power of God time and again because I prayed as the Spirit directed, and I know you can do the same. Can there be any better time than the present? What about this very moment?

❄

Quite often, Christian ministries and denominations issue a call to prayer, encouraging leaders to mobilize their people in concentrated prayer for the nation or for critical world situations. The president of the United States and many governors and mayors issue proclamations on the National Day of Prayer. These documents may mention prayer needs or give a prayer direction such as a call for repentance or seeking God's face. Such proclamations are often issued during times of crisis. For example, Abraham Lincoln proclaimed a Day of National Fasting and Prayer during the American Civil War.

Once the prayer effort has a direction, a movement's leaders can accelerate prayer in several ways. Let's look at four components of any successful prayer movement. They don't necessarily fall in this order but are usually present in each movement. (Small prayer movements like those within churches may not contain all four of the common elements. If you direct a small prayer group, you may want to look over these four components to see if your prayer strategies could be enhanced.)

MOBILIZATION

A movement of prayer cannot be effective unless it mobilizes its prayers to follow the direction of God's call. Conferences are great tools to accelerate this element. An example is the rallies and conferences organized each year by the National Day of Prayer throughout the United States. Other methods of mobilization are also used. Recently, a national call for prayer was issued in an ad in *USA Today*. This ad reached millions of people nationwide.

TRAINING

When people are called into battle, they need training. Sometimes this training is more effective when held prior to a large prayer conference so that the prayer battles during the event can be more effective. If the purpose of the event is to fast and pray, then you do not want to spend valuable time during the event having to train the attendees in the principles of prayer.

COMMUNICATION

During the Civil War, communication was a major problem for both the Union and Confederate armies. "Modern technology" consisted of messengers who carried out much of the communication. As a result, troops were occasionally sent to battle but found no enemy to fight. During the Battle of Gettysburg, Confederate General Robert E. Lee was frustrated by limited knowledge of Union troop deployment because his cavalry commander, J. E. B. Stuart, had taken his soldiers behind enemy lines. General Lee did not determine the strength and position of the enemy until after the battle had started.

Have you ever received a prayer request, prayed for it, then found out that God had answered the request months or days earlier? Perhaps you heard about a crisis and said, "If I would have known about it when it happened, I could have prayed for the situation." You may have felt left out of the battle action.

Sometimes, communication lines break down for unavoidable reasons, such as swiftly changing circumstances or the interference of spiritual enemy forces. But if a prayer movement is to gather momentum, it must establish good

---❖---

As God opens doors of opportunity for prayer, He will also help Spirit-filled intercessors develop effective deployment strategies.

---

communication so that people can prepare through prayer, battle in prayer, and thank God for victories. Therefore, prayer movements need to develop effective ways of communicating with the intercessors they mobilize.

Communication must include two kinds of information: specific, worthy needs and news of answers from God. Hearing up-to-date news will increase the intercessors' interest in praying for further needs.

DEPLOYMENT

Once intercessors are mobilized and trained, where should they be sent? What strategies will be used to gather people to pray?

Deployment strategies not only should fit the call given by God to the movement, but also should be developed to work effectively in the areas in which they will be used. The Lighthouse movement is a good example of deployment. Believers form "Lighthouses of Prayer" in their homes to pray for their neighborhoods. As more believers in an area form Lighthouses, neighborhoods and entire cities begin to feel the impact.

Mission America's goal is for believers to pray for every person in America. Part of its deployment strategy is prayer walking—walking through a neighborhood and praying for each home on each block.

As God opens doors of opportunity for prayer, He will also help Spirit-filled intercessors develop effective deployment strategies. Murmansk, Russia, is a city in the Arctic Circle. Because of extreme winter weather, prayer walking would not be an effective strategy. The intercessors developed a strategy they called the Mobilization Autobus Revival Strategy (MARS). Once a week, intercessors boarded an old bus at 5:30 in the morning. They drove to strategic places such as city hall or public schools, got out of the bus, and prayed for those institutions. In time, the strategy spread all over Russia. This is an example of how God can use many methods of deployment—perhaps even within one prayer movement.

THE PRAYER MOVEMENT UMBRELLA

In effective prayer movements, the four components depend on each other. If you send untrained troops into battle, many won't return because of discouragement. If you have trained troops, where will they go if there are no deployment strategies? Mobilization will be inadequate for the expanse of the call if not enough people are called out for the task at hand. If mobilized intercessors are not given timely prayer requests or hear the results of their prayers, they will lose heart.

Is God calling you to join or initiate a prayer movement? If so, the appendixes at the end of this book will help you get started.

———◆———

MAKE PRAYER A REGULAR, VITAL PART OF
YOUR DAILY SPIRITUAL LIFE.

————————

7

Live It!

Sometimes living the Christian life can be confusing. You may have even become bewildered with your prayer life or parts of it. The tips on prayer included in this book for your enrichment have been used by prayer warriors around the world. Make prayer a regular, vital part of your daily spiritual life.

ACTS

A good way to pray is by remembering A-C-T-S, or ACTS. ACTS is an acrostic that stands for Adoration, Confession, Thanksgiving, and Supplication. Although prayer cannot be reduced to a formula, these basic elements should be included in our communication with God.

Adoration

To adore God is to worship and praise Him, to honor and exalt Him in our hearts and minds and with our lips. Adoration expresses our complete trust in Him and reflects our confidence that He hears us. Adoration demonstrates our reverence, awe, love, and gratitude.

C onfession

When our discipline of prayer begins with adoration, the Holy Spirit has opportunity to reveal any sin in our life that needs to

be confessed. By seeing God in His purity, His holiness, and His love, we become aware of our own sinfulness and unworthiness. Confessing our sin and receiving His forgiveness restores us to fellowship with Him and clears the channel for God to hear and answer our prayers (1 John 1:7–9).

Nothing pleases God more than our consistent expression of faith.

T hanksgiving

Nothing pleases God more than our consistent expression of faith. What better way to do this than to tell Him "thank you?" God's Word commands, "No matter what happens, always be thankful, for this is God's will for you who belong to Christ Jesus" (1 Thessalonians 5:18). As we approach God with a thankful heart, He makes Himself strong on our behalf.

S upplication

Supplication includes petition for our own needs and intercession for others. We are to pray for everything and in specific terms.

These elements—adoration, confession, thanksgiving, and supplication—have helped many Christians to develop a more well-rounded prayer life.

GROUP PRAYER

We know we can and should pray privately, and God hears and answers. But if possible for you, it is also good to pray in groups of other believers, even if only one other person. There is special power in prayers of agreement and a special presence of the Lord.

Expect great things from God as you pray!

Expect great things from God as you pray! My desire is that this book would not simply make you more informed about prayer, but that it would help to make you a prayer warrior God can use mightily to advance His kingdom.

Readers' Guide

For Personal Reflection or Group Discussion

Questions are an inevitable part of life. Proud parents ask their new baby, "Can you smile?" Later they ask, "Can you say, 'Mama'?" "Can you walk to Daddy?" The early school years bring the inevitable, "What did you learn at school today?" Later school years introduce tougher questions, "If X equals 12 and Y equals –14, then … ?" Adulthood adds a whole new set of questions. "Should I remain single or marry?" "How did things go at the office?" "Did you get a raise?" "Should we let Susie start dating?" "Which college is right for Kyle?" "How can we possibly afford to send our kids to college?"

This book raises questions too. The following study guide is designed to (1) maximize the subject material and (2) apply biblical truth to daily life. You won't be asked to solve any algebraic problems or recall dates associated with obscure events in history, so relax. Questions asking for objective information are based solely on the text. Most questions, however, prompt you to search inside your soul, examine the circumstances that surround your life, and decide how you can best use the truths communicated in the book.

Honest answers to real issues can strengthen your faith, draw you closer to the Lord, and lead you into fuller, richer, more joyful, and productive daily adventures. So confront each question head-on and expect the One who is the answer for all of life's questions and needs to accomplish great things in your life.

CHAPTER 1: AN UNFATHOMABLE PRIVILEGE

1. How would you prepare for a conversation with the most powerful person on earth?

2. Why is holding a conversation with God vastly more important?

3. What does it mean to come boldly to God's throne? How does this invitation to come to God boldly affect your outlook on life?

4. Specifically, why do you need God's wisdom today?

5. How do believers demonstrate a commitment to prayer? What circumstances might increase this commitment?

CHAPTER 2: THE PURPOSE OF PRAYER

1. Realizing that God knows everything and is committed to meeting His people's needs, why should believers pray?

2. Believers should enter God's presence with a relaxed, joyful heart, according to Dr. Bright, but what circumstances might keep a believer from approaching God with such confidence?

3. How well do you appreciate the fact that you can pray directly to God any time and anywhere? What has been your most unusual place of prayer?

4. What is the major prerequisite to prayer? Will God answer an unbeliever's prayers? Why or why not?

5. What connection do you see between prayer and effective witnessing? How will you strengthen your prayer life this week?

Chapter 3: The Object of Prayer

1. Which of God's many perfect characteristics provides the most encouragement when you pray? Why?

2. What scriptural pattern for prayer involves the Persons of the Trinity?

3. How do Jesus' prayers inspire you to pray?

4. What aspects of public prayer encourage you? Frustrate you?

5. What answers to prayer have you seen? What answers do you want to see?

Chapter 4: The Power of Prayer

1. What does it mean to pray in the Spirit?

2. What impresses God: eloquent praying or humble praying? Why?

3. Do you agree or disagree that reverence is a jewel that is often missing from prayer? Defend your answer.

4. Why is it important to be transparent when we talk to God?

5. Dr. Bright observes, "We do not serve a God of convenience but a God of perfect timing." How have you found this observation to be true?

CHAPTER 5: PRAYING WITH CONFIDENCE

1. Why do we sometimes doubt God's willingness or His power to answer our prayers?

2. How does an unforgiving spirit affect prayer?

3. What four words does the author suggest that can help us to pray confidently?

4. Does the possibility exist that God may grow tired of our asking? Why or why not?

5. What means does the Spirit use to produce faith in those who pray? Which, if any, of these means do you need to heed more fully?

CHAPTER 6: BELIEVING GOD FOR THE GREAT COMMISSION

1. How can believers pray effectively for world evangelization?

2. Who or what will you claim for God as you pray this week?

3. To what does Dr. Bright credit the impotence and lack of fruitfulness he observes among Christians? Why do you agree or disagree with his observation?

4. How does today's world compare with the first-century world? Is our world harder to evangelize? Why or why not?

5. To what extent do you believe a National Day of Prayer effectively advances the cause of Christ? How might it become more effective?

CHAPTER 7: LIVE IT!

1. What tips for prayer does Dr. Bright offer in the form of the acrostic, "ACTS"?

2. How can a believer be truly thankful in the midst of adversity? What does every Christian have to be thankful for?

3. How does supplication differ from asking?

4. What advantages do you see in group prayer?

5. How can your life be enriched through prayer?

Appendix A

God's Promises and Prevailing Prayer

UNDERSTAND CONDITIONAL PROMISES

Identify the condition and promise in each of the following verses:

1. Jeremiah 33:3 (NIV): "Call to me and I will answer you and tell you great and unsearchable things you do not know."
   Condition:
   Promise:

2. Matthew 21:22: "If you believe, you will receive whatever you ask for in prayer."
   Condition:
   Promise:

3. First John 5:14–15 (NIV): "This is the confidence we have in approaching God: that if we ask anything according to his will, he hears us. And if we know that he hears us— whatever we ask—we know that we have what we asked of him."

Condition:

Promise:

4. John 14:14 (NIV): "You may ask me for anything in my name, and I will do it."

Condition:

Promise:

Which promise do you need most to apply to your own prayer life right now and why?

EMBRACE GOD'S PROMISES

1. For material needs
   - Philippians 4:19 (NIV): "And my God will meet all your needs according to his glorious riches in Christ Jesus."
   - Psalm 84:11: "For the LORD God is our light and protector. He gives us grace and glory. No good thing will the LORD withhold from those who do what is right."

2. For guidance
   - Proverbs 3:5–6: "Trust in the LORD with all your heart; do not depend on your own understanding. Seek his will in all you do, and he will direct your paths."
   - Psalm 32:8: "The LORD says, 'I will guide you along the best pathway for your life. I will advise you and watch over you.'"

3. For spiritual needs
   - Ephesians 1:3: "How we praise God, the Father of our Lord Jesus Christ, who has blessed us with every spiritual

blessing in the heavenly realms because we belong to Christ."

- Philippians 4:13: "For I can do everything with the help of Christ who gives me the strength I need."

REASONS YOU CAN TRUST GOD TO KEEP HIS PROMISES

These promises are real—believe them; claim them; live by them!

- Psalm 9:10: "Those who know your name trust in you, for you, O LORD, have never abandoned anyone who searches for you."
- Psalm 115:11: "All you who fear the LORD, trust the LORD! He is your helper; he is your shield."
- Isaiah 26:4:"Trust in the LORD always, for the LORD GOD is the eternal Rock."
- Nahum 1:7: "The LORD is good. When trouble comes, he is a strong refuge. And he knows everyone who trusts in him."
- 2 Samuel 7:28: "For you are God, O Sovereign LORD. Your words are truth, and you have promised these good things to me, your servant."

In what particular circumstance of your life do you presently need to trust Him more—and for what?

CONDITIONS TO ANSWERED PRAYER

1. Why is it necessary to ask in accordance with the will of God?

    "And we can be confident that he will listen to us whenever we ask him for anything in line with his will. And if we know he is listening when we make our requests, we can be sure that he will give us what we ask for" (1 John 5:14–15).

2. Write out John 15:7 in your own words and state what it teaches about conditions to answered prayer.

"But if you stay joined to me and my words remain in you, you may ask any request you like, and it will be granted!"

3. What is the value of several Christians praying for something as opposed to just one?

"I also tell you this: If two of you agree down here on earth concerning anything you ask, my Father in heaven will do it for you" (Matthew 18:19).

PREVAILING PRAYER

During his lifetime, George Müeller recorded more than 50,000 answers to prayer. He prayed for two men daily for more than sixty years. One of these men was converted shortly before Müeller's death and the other about a year later. As in Müeller's experience, we do not always see the answers to our prayers right away. We must be persistent and patient with God.

1. How long do you think we should pray for someone or something (see Luke 18:1–8)? Why do you think God honors prevailing prayer? What part do our feelings play in prevailing prayer?

"One day Jesus told his disciples a story to illustrate their need for constant prayer and to show them that they must never give up" (Luke 18:1).

2. What did the following men accomplish through prayer?

How do these examples help you gain greater confidence to pray? Give an example of what God has done for you or someone you know as the result of prevailing prayer.

- MOSES (Exodus 15:22–26)

  Then Moses led the people of Israel away from the Red Sea, and they moved out into the Shur Desert. They traveled in this desert for three days without water. When they came to Marah, they finally found water. But the people couldn't drink it because it was bitter. (That is why the place was called Marah, which means "bitter.")

  Then the people turned against Moses. "What are we going to drink?" they demanded.

  So Moses cried out to the LORD for help, and the LORD showed him a branch. Moses took the branch and threw it into the water. This made the water good to drink.

  It was there at Marah that the LORD laid before them the following conditions to test their faithfulness to him: "If you will listen carefully to the voice of the LORD your God and do what is right in his sight, obeying his commands and laws, then I will not make you suffer the diseases I sent on the Egyptians; for I am the LORD who heals you."

- SAMSON (Judges 16:28–30)

  Then Samson prayed to the LORD, "Sovereign LORD, remember me again. O God, please strengthen me one more time so that I may pay back the Philistines for the loss of my eyes." Then Samson put his hands on the center pillars of the temple and pushed against them with all his might. "Let me die with the Philistines," he prayed. And the temple crashed down on the Philistine leaders and all the people. So he killed more people when he died than he had during his entire lifetime.

- PETER (Acts 9:36–41)

  There was a believer in Joppa named Tabitha (which in Greek is Dorcas). She was always doing kind things for others and helping the poor. About this time she became ill and died. Her friends prepared her for burial and laid her in an upstairs room. But they had heard that Peter was nearby at Lydda, so they sent two men to beg him, "Please come as soon as possible!"

  So Peter returned with them; and as soon as he arrived, they took him to the upstairs room. The room was filled with widows who were weeping and showing him the coats and other garments Dorcas had made for them. But Peter asked them all to leave the room; then he knelt and prayed. Turning to the body he said, "Get up, Tabitha." And she opened her eyes! When she saw Peter, she sat up! He gave her his hand and helped her up. Then he called in the widows and all the believers, and he showed them that she was alive.

- ELIJAH (James 5:17–18)

  Elijah was as human as we are, and yet when he prayed earnestly that no rain would fall, none fell for the next three and a half years! Then he prayed for rain, and down it poured. The grass turned green, and the crops began to grow again.

Appendix B

Plan Your Prayer Time

Y ou may pray throughout the day. However, many Christians experience special times of prayer while fellow-shipping with God in their devotions. If you do not have a regular time for devotions, here are some steps to begin. Take time to interact with the verses and questions that follow.

ESTABLISH A DEFINITE TIME

A daily devotional time should be set aside for personal worship and meditation in which we seek fellowship with the Lord Jesus Christ.

1. What do these verses tell us about the importance of taking time to be with God?

Oh, how I love your law! I think about it all day long.

PSALM 119:97

Keep on praying.

1 THESSALONIANS 5:17

2. In obedience to Christ's command, what did the disciples do after His ascension?

> Then they went to the upstairs room of the house where they were staying. Here is the list of those who were present: Peter, John, James, Andrew, Philip, Thomas, Bartholomew, Matthew, James (son of Alphaeus), Simon (the Zealot), and Judas (son of James).
>
> They all met together continually for prayer, along with Mary the mother of Jesus, several other women, and the brothers of Jesus.
>
> ACTS 1:13–14

3. Although individual schedules will vary, many people prefer to have their devotional time in the morning hours, before the responsibilities of the day begin. David was called a man after God's own heart. What time did he set aside to communicate with God?

> Listen to my voice in the morning, LORD. Each morning I bring my requests to you and wait expectantly.
>
> PSALM 5:3

4. List two characteristics of the devotional life of Jesus.

> The next morning Jesus awoke long before daybreak and went out alone into the wilderness to pray.
>
> MARK 1:35

5. When is your best devotional time? None of us can say that we do not have time for prayer and Bible study. We all can make time for things that we really want to do. Whether the period is long or short, set aside some time.

6. Make your devotional time unhurried. Don't think about your next responsibility. Concentrate on your fellowship with the Lord. A definite time every day will do much to help. A brief period with concentration is better than a long devotional time with your mind on many things. How many minutes can you set aside daily for your time with God?

Choose a Definite Place

Avoid distraction by finding a quiet, private place of worship. If privacy is impossible, you will need to concentrate. If you cannot have a devotional time in your own home or room, perhaps one of the following places will be suitable:

- A nearby chapel
- A corner of the school library
- Your office (before or after hours)

List three other places you might find appropriate for your private prayer and Bible study.

1.
2.
3.

Understand the Goal and Content of Your Devotional Time

We should have a reason for everything we do. "Aim at nothing and you will surely hit it." Our purpose for prayer should be to establish a personal fellowship with God and to fulfill our own spiritual needs.

A brief time of meeting with God in the early morning and walking in vital union with Him throughout the day, "practicing the presence of God," is more meaningful than spending an hour or more in a legalistic way and forgetting Him for the rest of the day.

1. During our devotional time, we should be concerned with learning where we have failed and with rededicating ourselves to the task before us. We should use the time to regroup our forces after the battles of the previous day and plan for the coming day's attack.

   • What particular need do you feel today?

   • What battles did you have yesterday?

2. The devotional time should include Bible study, prayer, personal worship, and quiet meditation. These aspects of the devotional time are so closely related that you can actually engage in all at the same time.

   For example, begin by reading a psalm of thanksgiving or praise. As you read, your heart will respond, and you will continue to praise and worship God from a grateful heart.

   Turn now to another portion of Scripture, such as Romans 2. Interrupt your reading to thank God for each truth that applies to you as a Christian. You will be amazed at how much you have to praise and thank God for, once you get started.

   After you have read and prayed for a while, remain in an attitude of quiet, listening for instructions from God. Write down any thoughts that come to mind, and pray about these.

Supplementary activity may include memorizing Scripture or reading from a devotional book or hymnal.

3. Paraphrase the following prayer from Matthew 6:9–13, using expressions meaningful to you.

Pray like this: Our Father in heaven, may your name be honored. May your Kingdom come soon. May your will be done here on earth, just as it is in heaven. Give us our food for today, and forgive us our sins, just as we have forgiven those who have sinned against us. And don't let us yield to temptation, but deliver us from the evil one.

Perhaps you have a burden to pray for specific things. Appendix C offers some topics and appendix D lists Scripture passages that may be helpful.

GIVE ALL YOUR WORRIES AND CARES TO GOD,
FOR HE CARES ABOUT WHAT HAPPENS TO YOU.

1 PETER 5:7

Appendix C

Prayer Topics

CALL FOR REVIVAL

- Thank God for His omniscience and power to bring revival.
- Pray that there will be a great spiritual awakening across America and the world.
- Pray that we will confess our sin as God sees it.
- Ask God for repentance for our lack of deeper involvement in society.
- Ask God to bless the women's prayer movement and that men will also have a burden for prayer.
- Pray for sweeping movements of evangelism and awakening among our youth.

THE CHURCH

- Thank God for the religious freedom we enjoy.
- Pray that the church will yield completely to God and His refiner's fire.
- Pray that the church will return to its place of leadership in society.

- Pray that pastors and evangelists will have a commitment to live and teach the truth.
- Pray that we will love each other in the church.
- Pray for racial reconciliation within the church.
- Pray that believers will have a unity and will not quarrel among themselves.
- Pray that we will have a burden for evangelism.
- Pray that thousands of new churches will open.
- Pray for the persecuted church around the world and that American believers will speak up on their behalf.
- Pray for salvation of those who persecute the church.
- Pray that the church will be ready when the harvest comes.

FELLOW CHRISTIANS

- Pray that we will reflect the love of Christ.
- Pray that we will experience revival in the body of Christ.
- Pray that we will boldly proclaim God's Word and call sin, sin.
- Pray that we will have a hunger for holiness despite the cost.
- Thank God for our brothers and sisters in Christ.
- Pray that we will avoid deception and the cares of this life.
- Pray that all people will have moral courage and integrity.
- Pray for single parents and for grandparents who are raising their grandchildren.

THE WORLD

- Thank God for the work His Spirit is doing on every continent.

- Pray for the two billion persons who have yet to hear of Jesus' name.
- Ask God to send out laborers into the harvest.

FAMILIES AND CHILDREN

- Thank God for families that honor and obey Him.
- Pray for revival and reformation in homes across our country.
- Pray that Christian families will have God's direction and sufficient resources.
- Pray for the sixty-two million children in the United States.
- Pray that government leaders will be granted wisdom to encourage and support the family.
- Pray that men and women will make their homes their priority.

THE WORLDWIDE OUTREACH OF THE CHURCH

- Praise God for the opportunity we have to reach out to people around the world with the gospel.
- Pray that God's Word will be made available for every people group.
- Pray that the Word of God will reach places where Scripture presently cannot be distributed.

BEYOND THE WALLS OF THE CHURCH

- Thank God for the many Christians who serve Him in all parts of secular society.
- Pray that God will cause hearts to burn with a desire to share the good news of Christ in neighborhoods, offices, and social settings.

- Pray that we will become aware of the daily opportunities God brings our way to share the gospel.
- Pray that we will weep over our cities as Christ wept over Jerusalem.
- Pray for servicemen and -women who serve our country throughout the world.
- Pray for prison ministries, the largest mission field in our country.
- Pray for Christians in secular journalism.

LEADERS IN SOCIETY

- Thank God for the Christian leaders who are faithfully serving Him despite the cost.
- Pray for our
  - president and vice president
  - congressional leaders
  - U.S. Supreme Court
  - governors and state legislators
  - federal and state judges
  - city government officials
  - school boards
- Pray that local and national spiritual leaders will not waver but will finish strong.
- Pray that more dedicated young Christians will accept leadership roles in all areas of society.
- Pray that government leaders will speak the truth and seek godly wisdom in decision making.
- Pray that teachers, professors, and administrators will seek and proclaim the truth.
- Pray that believers on college campuses will boldly proclaim Jesus and live godly lives.

- Pray for the salvation and discipleship of more than 500,000 international students on American campuses.

———◆———

AND YOU WILL ALWAYS GIVE THANKS FOR
EVERYTHING TO GOD THE FATHER IN THE NAME OF
OUR LORD JESUS CHRIST.

EPHESIANS 5:20

———————

Appendix D

Scriptures for Prayer

U sing Scripture during your prayer time can help you pray more specifically and according to God's will.

PRAY FOR YOURSELF

Pray for pure thoughts and deeds, that you may be a channel for God's love where you live, work, and worship.

So we have continued praying for you ever since we first heard about you. We ask God to give you a complete understanding of what he wants to do in your lives, and we ask him to make you wise with spiritual wisdom. Then the way you live will always honor and please the Lord, and you will continually do good, kind things for others. All the while, you will learn to know God better and better.

We also pray that you will be strengthened with his glorious power so that you will have all the patience and endurance you need. May you be filled with joy, always thanking the Father, who has enabled you to share the inheritance that belongs to God's holy people, who live in the light.

COLOSSIANS 1:9–12

And now, dear brothers and sisters, let me say one more thing as I close this letter. Fix your thoughts on what is true and honorable and right. Think about things that are pure and lovely and admirable. Think about things that are excellent and worthy of praise.

PHILIPPIANS 4:8

But thanks be to God, who made us his captives and leads us along in Christ's triumphal procession. Now wherever we go he uses us to tell others about the Lord and to spread the Good News like a sweet perfume.

2 CORINTHIANS 2:14

So think clearly and exercise self-control. Look forward to the special blessings that will come to you at the return of Jesus Christ. Obey God because you are his children. Don't slip back into your old ways of doing evil; you didn't know any better then. But now you must be holy in everything you do, just as God—who chose you to be his children—is holy. For he himself has said, "You must be holy because I am holy."

1 PETER 1:13–16

PRAY FOR YOUR HOME AND FAMILY

Pray for a Christ-centered home and family. Seek God's wisdom and guidance in applying His principles.

Get rid of all bitterness, rage, anger, harsh words, and slander, as well as all types of malicious behavior. Instead, be kind to each other, tenderhearted, forgiving one another, just as God through Christ has forgiven you.

EPHESIANS 4:31–32

You wives will submit to your husbands as you do to the Lord.

EPHESIANS 5:22

And now a word to you fathers. Don't make your children angry by the way you treat them. Rather, bring them up with the discipline and instruction approved by the Lord.

EPHESIANS 6:4

Finally, all of you should be of one mind, full of sympathy toward each other, loving one another with tender hearts and humble minds. Don't repay evil for evil. Don't retaliate when people say unkind things about you. Instead, pay them back with a blessing. That is what God wants you to do, and he will bless you for it.

1 PETER 3:8–9

The curse of the LORD is on the house of the wicked, but his blessing is on the home of the upright.

PROVERBS 3:33

Unless the LORD builds a house, the work of the builders is useless. Unless the LORD protects a city, guarding it with sentries will do no good.

PSALM 127:1

PRAY FOR THE CHURCH

Pray for unity within the church and Christian organizations. Pray that believers will witness for Christ through their lives and words.

Is there any encouragement from belonging to Christ? Any comfort from his love? Any fellowship together in the Spirit? Are your hearts tender and sympathetic? Then make me truly happy by agreeing wholeheartedly with each other, loving one another, and working together with one heart and purpose.

Don't be selfish; don't live to make a good impression on others. Be humble, thinking of others as better than yourself. Don't think only about your own affairs, but be interested in others, too, and what they are doing.

Your attitude should be the same that Christ Jesus had. Though he was God, he did not demand and cling to his rights as God. He made himself nothing; he took the humble position of a slave and appeared in human form.

PHILIPPIANS 2:1–7

"Now I am departing the world; I am leaving them behind and coming to you. Holy Father, keep them and care for them—all those you have given me—so that they will be united just as we are."

JOHN 17:11

Therefore I, a prisoner for serving the Lord, beg you to
lead a life worthy of your calling, for you have been called
by God. Be humble and gentle. Be patient with each other,
making allowance for each other's faults because of your
love. Always keep yourselves united in the Holy Spirit, and
bind yourselves together with peace.

EPHESIANS 4:1–3

He is the one who gave these gifts to the church: the apostles, the prophets, the evangelists, and the pastors and
teachers. Their responsibility is to equip God's people to do
his work and build up the church, the body of Christ, until
we come to such unity in our faith and knowledge of God's
Son that we will be mature and full grown in the Lord,
measuring up to the full stature of Christ.

Then we will no longer be like children, forever
changing our minds about what we believe because
someone has told us something different or because
someone has cleverly lied to us and made the lie sound
like the truth. Instead, we will hold to the truth in love,
becoming more and more in every way like Christ, who
is the head of his body, the church. Under his direction,
the whole body is fitted together perfectly. As each part
does its own special work, it helps the other parts grow,
so that the whole body is healthy and growing and full
of love.

EPHESIANS 4:11–16

The human body has many parts, but the many parts
make up only one body. So it is with the body of Christ.

99

Some of us are Jews, some are Gentiles, some are slaves, and some are free. But we have all been baptized into Christ's body by one Spirit, and we have all received the same Spirit.

1 CORINTHIANS 12:12–13

But thanks be to God, who made us his captives and leads us along in Christ's triumphal procession. Now wherever we go he uses us to tell others about the Lord and to spread the Good News like a sweet perfume. Our lives are a fragrance presented by Christ to God. But this fragrance is perceived differently by those being saved and by those perishing. To those who are perishing we are a fearful smell of death and doom. But to those who are being saved we are a life-giving perfume. And who is adequate for such a task as this? You see, we are not like those hucksters— and there are many of them—who preach just to make money. We preach God's message with sincerity and with Christ's authority. And we know that the God who sent us is watching us.

2 CORINTHIANS 2:14–17

Whatever we do, it is because Christ's love controls us. Since we believe that Christ died for everyone, we also believe that we have all died to the old life we used to live. He died for everyone so that those who receive his new life will no longer live to please themselves. Instead, they will live to please Christ, who died and was raised for them.

So we have stopped evaluating others by what the world thinks about them. Once I mistakenly thought of

Christ that way, as though he were merely a human being. How differently I think about him now! What this means is that those who become Christians become new persons. They are not the same anymore, for the old life is gone. A new life has begun!

All this newness of life is from God, who brought us back to himself through what Christ did. And God has given us the task of reconciling people to him. For God was in Christ, reconciling the world to himself, no longer counting people's sins against them. This is the wonderful message he has given us to tell others. We are Christ's ambassadors, and God is using us to speak to you. We urge you, as though Christ himself were here pleading with you, "Be reconciled to God!" For God made Christ, who never sinned, to be the offering for our sin, so that we could be made right with God through Christ.

2 CORINTHIANS 5:14–21

PRAY FOR YOUR COMMUNITY

Pray for a Christian ministry of reconciliation in your community.

Don't think only of your own good. Think of other Christians and what is best for them.

1 CORINTHIANS 10:24

But thanks be to God, who made us his captives and leads us along in Christ's triumphal procession. Now wherever we go he uses us to tell others about the Lord and to spread the Good News like a sweet perfume. Our lives are a fragrance presented by Christ to God. But this fragrance is perceived differently by those being saved and by those perishing. To those who are perishing we are a fearful smell of death and doom. But to those who are being saved we are a life-giving perfume. And who is adequate for such a task as this?

2 CORINTHIANS 2:14–16

It is not that we think we can do anything of lasting value by ourselves. Our only power and success come from God.

2 CORINTHIANS 3:5

What this means is that those who become Christians become new persons. They are not the same anymore, for the old life is gone. A new life has begun!

All this newness of life is from God, who brought us back to himself through what Christ did. And God has given us the task of reconciling people to him. For God was in Christ, reconciling the world to himself, no longer counting people's sins against them. This is the wonderful message he has given us to tell others. We are Christ's ambassadors, and God is using us to speak to you. We urge you, as though Christ himself were here pleading with you, "Be reconciled to God!"

2 CORINTHIANS 5:17–20

"Ask me and I will tell you some remarkable secrets about what is going to happen here. For this is what the LORD, the God of Israel, says: Though you have torn down the houses of this city and even the king's palace to get materials to strengthen the walls against the siege weapons of the enemy, the Babylonians will still enter. The men of this city are already as good as dead, for I have determined to destroy them in my terrible anger. I have abandoned them because of all their wickedness.

"Nevertheless, the time will come when I will heal Jerusalem's damage and give her prosperity and peace. I will restore the fortunes of Judah and Israel and rebuild their cities. I will cleanse away their sins against me, and I will forgive all their sins of rebellion."

JEREMIAH 33:3–8

Unless the LORD builds a house, the work of the builders is useless. Unless the LORD protects a city, guarding it with sentries will do no good.

PSALM 127:1

PRAY FOR YOUR NATION

Pray for national repentance, acknowledging God's mercy and forgiveness.

Then if my people who are called by my name will humble themselves and pray and seek my face and turn from their wicked ways, I will hear from heaven and will forgive their sins and heal their land.

2 CHRONICLES 7:14

"So you see, God is with us. He is our leader. His priests blow their trumpets and lead us into battle against you. O people of Israel, do not fight against the LORD, the God of your ancestors, for you will not succeed!"

2 CHRONICLES 13:12

And he went out to meet King Asa as he was returning from the battle. "Listen to me, Asa!" he shouted. "Listen, all you people of Judah and Benjamin! The LORD will stay with you as long as you stay with him! Whenever you seek him, you will find him. But if you abandon him, he will abandon you."

2 CHRONICLES 15:2

Jehoshaphat was alarmed by this news and sought the LORD for guidance. He also gave orders that everyone throughout Judah should observe a fast. So people from all the towns of Judah came to Jerusalem to seek the LORD.

Jehoshaphat stood before the people of Judah and Jerusalem in front of the new courtyard at the Temple of the LORD. He prayed, "O LORD, God of our ancestors, you alone are the God who is in heaven. You are ruler of all the kingdoms of the earth. You are powerful and mighty; no one can stand against you!"

2 CHRONICLES 20:3-6

"O our God, won't you stop them? We are powerless against this mighty army that is about to attack us. We do not know what to do, but we are looking to you for help."

2 CHRONICLES 20:12

Then the Spirit of God came upon Zechariah son of Jehoiada the priest. He stood before the people and said, "This is what God says: Why do you disobey the

LORD's commands so that you cannot prosper? You have abandoned the LORD, and now he has abandoned you!"

2 CHRONICLES 24:20

At the same time, God's hand was on the people in the land of Judah, giving them a strong desire to unite in obeying the orders of the king and his officials, who were following the word of the LORD.

2 CHRONICLES 30:12

"Have you seen this, son of man?" he asked. "Is it nothing to the people of Judah that they commit these terrible sins, leading the whole nation into violence, thumbing their noses at me, and rousing my fury against them? Therefore, I will deal with them in fury. I will neither pity nor spare them. And though they scream for mercy, I will not listen."

EZEKIEL 8:17-18

And there by the Ahava Canal, I gave orders for all of us to fast and humble ourselves before our God. We prayed that he would give us a safe journey and protect us, our children, and our goods as we traveled. For I was ashamed to ask the king for soldiers and horsemen to accompany us and protect us from enemies along the way. After all, we had told the king, "Our God protects all those who worship him, but his fierce anger rages against those who abandon him." So we fasted and earnestly prayed that our God would take care of us, and he heard our prayer.

EZRA 8:21-23

PRAY FOR THE WORLD

Pray for a spirit of revival to sweep the world, that the nations will worship the Lord with reverence.

Why do the nations rage? Why do the people waste their time with futile plans? The kings of the earth prepare for battle; the rulers plot together against the LORD and against his anointed one. "Let us break their chains," they cry, "and free ourselves from this slavery."

But the one who rules in heaven laughs. The Lord scoffs at them. Then in anger he rebukes them, terrifying them with his fierce fury. For the LORD declares, "I have placed my chosen king on the throne in Jerusalem, my holy city."

The king proclaims the LORD's decree: "The LORD said to me, 'You are my son. Today I have become your Father. Only ask, and I will give you the nations as your inheritance, the ends of the earth as your possession. You will break them with an iron rod and smash them like clay pots.'"

Now then, you kings, act wisely! Be warned, you rulers of the earth! Serve the LORD with reverent fear, and rejoice with trembling. Submit to God's royal son, or he will become angry, and you will be destroyed in the midst of your pursuits—for his anger can flare up in an instant.

But what joy for all who find protection in him!

PSALM 2

Let everyone in the world fear the LORD, and let everyone stand in awe of him.

PSALM 33:8

The LORD shatters the plans of the nations and thwarts all
their schemes. But the LORD's plans stand firm forever; his
intentions can never be shaken.

What joy for the nation whose God is the LORD, whose
people he has chosen for his own.

PSALM 33:10–12

PRAY FOR THOSE IN AUTHORITY

Pray that the leaders of our country will have wisdom, integrity,
protection, and guidance.

But some teachers have missed this whole point. They have
turned away from these things and spend their time
arguing and talking foolishness.

1 TIMOTHY 1:6

I urge you, first of all, to pray for all people. As you make
your requests, plead for God's mercy upon them, and give
thanks. Pray this way for kings and all others who are in
authority, so that we can live in peace and quietness, in
godliness and dignity. This is good and pleases God our
Savior, for he wants everyone to be saved and to understand the truth. For there is only one God and one
Mediator who can reconcile God and people. He is the
man Christ Jesus. He gave his life to purchase freedom for
everyone. This is the message that God gave to the world
at the proper time.

1 TIMOTHY 2:1–6

I did this so that you might trust the power of God rather than human wisdom.

1 CORINTHIANS 2:5

Stop fooling yourselves. If you think you are wise by this world's standards, you will have to become a fool so you can become wise by God's standards. For the wisdom of this world is foolishness to God. As the Scriptures say,

"God catches those who think they are wise in their own cleverness."

And again,

"The Lord knows the thoughts of the wise, that they are worthless."

1 CORINTHIANS 3:18–20

Obey the government, for God is the one who put it there. All governments have been placed in power by God.

ROMANS 13:1

"Now if you will fear and worship the LORD and listen to his voice, and if you do not rebel against the LORD's commands, and if you and your king follow the LORD your God, then all will be well. But if you rebel against the LORD's commands and refuse to listen to him, then his hand will be as heavy upon you as it was upon your ancestors."

1 SAMUEL 12:14–15

"Ask me and I will tell you some remarkable secrets about what is going to happen here."

JEREMIAH 33:3

PRAY FOR NONBELIEVERS

Pray that the lost will be freed from the Enemy, enlightened through the gospel, granted repentance, and drawn to the Father.

I speak this way, using the illustration of slaves and masters, because it is easy to understand. Before, you let yourselves be slaves of impurity and lawlessness. Now you must choose to be slaves of righteousness so that you will become holy.

In those days, when you were slaves of sin, you weren't concerned with doing what was right. And what was the result? It was not good, since now you are ashamed of the things you used to do, things that end in eternal doom. But now you are free from the power of sin and have become slaves of God. Now you do those things that lead to holiness and result in eternal life. For the wages of sin is death, but the free gift of God is eternal life through Christ Jesus our Lord.

ROMANS 6:19–23

Dear brothers and sisters, the longing of my heart and my prayer to God is that the Jewish people might be saved.

ROMANS 10:1

For "Anyone who calls on the name of the Lord will be saved."

But how can they call on him to save them unless they believe in him? And how can they believe in him if they have never heard about him? And how can they hear about him unless someone tells them? And how will anyone go and tell them without being sent? That is what the Scriptures mean when they say, "How beautiful are the feet of those who bring good news!"

ROMANS 10:13–15

For he wants everyone to be saved and to understand the truth. For there is only one God and one Mediator who can reconcile God and people. He is the man Christ Jesus. He gave his life to purchase freedom for everyone. This is the message that God gave to the world at the proper time.

1 TIMOTHY 2:4–6

They should gently teach those who oppose the truth. Perhaps God will change those people's hearts, and they will believe the truth. Then they will come to their senses and escape from the Devil's trap. For they have been held captive by him to do whatever he wants.

2 TIMOTHY 2:25–26

"Look! Here I stand at the door and knock. If you hear me calling and open the door, I will come in, and we will share a meal as friends."

REVELATION 3:20

"So if the Son sets you free, you will indeed be free."

JOHN 8:36

Now, the Lord is the Spirit, and wherever the Spirit of the Lord is, he gives freedom.

2 CORINTHIANS 3:17

PRAY FOR THE SICK, DISCOURAGED, AND PERSECUTED

Pray for God's mercy, strength, and loving-kindness. Pray that they may be aware of His presence.

"The name of Jesus has healed this man—and you know how lame he was before. Faith in Jesus' name has caused this healing before your very eyes."

ACTS 3:16

And he surely was ill; in fact, he almost died. But God had mercy on him—and also on me, so that I would not have such unbearable sorrow.

PHILIPPIANS 2:27

Are any among you sick? They should call for the elders of the church and have them pray over them, anointing them with oil in the name of the Lord. And their prayer offered in faith will heal the sick, and the Lord will make them well. And anyone who has committed sins will be forgiven.

JAMES 5:14–15

Give all your worries and cares to God, for he cares about
what happens to you.

1 PETER 5:7

May God our Father and the Lord Jesus Christ give you
his grace and peace.

I can never stop thanking God for all the generous gifts
he has given you, now that you belong to Christ Jesus.

1 CORINTHIANS 1:3-4

So I ask you to follow my example and do as I do.

That is the very reason I am sending Timothy—to help
you do this. For he is my beloved and trustworthy child in
the Lord. He will remind you of what I teach about Christ
Jesus in all the churches wherever I go.

1 CORINTHIANS 4:16-17

To one person the Spirit gives the ability to give wise
advice; to another he gives the gift of special knowledge.
The Spirit gives special faith to another, and to someone
else he gives the power to heal the sick. He gives one
person the power to perform miracles, and to another the
ability to prophesy. He gives someone else the ability to
know whether it is really the Spirit of God or another spirit
that is speaking. Still another person is given the ability to
speak in unknown languages, and another is given the
ability to interpret what is being said.

1 CORINTHIANS 12:8-10

In my distress I prayed to the LORD, and the LORD
answered me and rescued me. The LORD is for me, so I
will not be afraid. What can mere mortals do to me?

PSALM 118:5–6

And you will always give thanks for everything to God the
Father in the name of our Lord Jesus Christ.

EPHESIANS 5:20

PRAY FOR THE MEDIA

Pray for Christian influence in newspapers, magazines, television, and movies.

Don't let anyone lead you astray with empty philosophy
and high-sounding nonsense that come from human
thinking and from the evil powers of this world, and not
from Christ.

COLOSSIANS 2:8

Fear of the LORD is the beginning of knowledge. Only
fools despise wisdom and discipline....

PROVERBS 1:7

The LORD despises the thoughts of the wicked, but he
delights in pure words.
The godly think before speaking; the wicked spout evil
words....
If you listen to constructive criticism, you will be at
home among the wise.

PROVERBS 15:26, 28, 31

PRAY FOR STUDENTS AND TEACHERS

Pray for teachers to teach biblical principles and values and for students to honor the Lord through pure lives.

> So please don't despair because of what they are doing to me here. It is for you that I am suffering, so you should feel honored and encouraged.
>
> When I think of the wisdom and scope of God's plan, I fall to my knees and pray to the Father, the Creator of everything in heaven and on earth. I pray that from his glorious, unlimited resources he will give you mighty inner strength through his Holy Spirit. And I pray that Christ will be more and more at home in your hearts as you trust in him. May your roots go down deep into the soil of God's marvelous love. And may you have the power to understand, as all God's people should, how wide, how long, how high, and how deep his love really is. May you experience the love of Christ, though it is so great you will never fully understand it. Then you will be filled with the fullness of life and power that comes from God.
>
> EPHESIANS 3:13–19

Follow God's example in everything you do, because you are his dear children. Live a life filled with love for others, following the example of Christ, who loved you and gave himself as a sacrifice to take away your sins. And God was pleased, because that sacrifice was like sweet perfume to him.

Let there be no sexual immorality, impurity, or greed among you. Such sins have no place among God's people.

Obscene stories, foolish talk, and coarse jokes—these are not for you. Instead, let there be thankfulness to God.

EPHESIANS 5:1-4

Oh, the joys of those who do not follow the advice of the wicked, or stand around with sinners, or join in with scoffers. But they delight in doing everything the LORD wants; day and night they think about his law. They are like trees planted along the riverbank, bearing fruit each season without fail. Their leaves never wither, and in all they do, they prosper.

PSALM 1:1-3

You will show me the way of life, granting me the joy of your presence and the pleasures of living with you forever.

PSALM 16:11

The steps of the godly are directed by the LORD. He delights in every detail of their lives. Though they stumble, they will not fall, for the LORD holds them by the hand.

PSALM 37:23-24

—————◆—————

THE LONGER I FASTED,
THE MORE I SENSED THE PRESENCE OF THE LORD.

—————————————

Appendix E

Seven Basic Steps
to Successful Fasting

I believe the power of fasting as it relates to prayer is the spiritual atomic bomb that our Lord has given us to destroy the strongholds of evil and usher in a great revival and spiritual harvest around the world.

Increasingly I have been gripped with a growing sense of urgency to call upon God to send revival to our beloved country. In the spring and summer of 1994, I had a growing conviction that God wanted me to fast and pray for forty days for revival in America and for the fulfillment of the Great Commission in obedience to our Lord's command.

At first I questioned, "Is this truly God's call for me?" Forty days was a long time to go without solid food. But with each passing day, His call grew stronger and clearer. Finally, I was convinced. God was calling me to fast, and He would not make such a call without a specific reason or purpose. With this conviction, I entered my fast with excitement and expectancy mounting in my heart, praying, "Lord, what do You want me to do?"

I believe such a long fast was a sovereign call of God

because of the magnitude of the sins of America and of the church. The Lord impressed that upon my heart, as well as the urgent need to help accelerate the fulfillment of the Great Commission in this generation.

As I began my fast, I was not sure I could continue for forty days. But my confidence was in the Lord to help me. Each day His presence encouraged me to continue. The longer I fasted, the more I sensed the presence of the Lord. The Holy Spirit refreshed my soul and spirit, and I experienced the joy of the Lord as seldom before. Biblical truths leaped at me from the pages of God's Word. My faith soared as I humbled myself and cried out to God and rejoiced in His presence.

How you begin and conduct your fast will largely determine your success. By following these seven basic steps to fasting, you will make your time with the Lord more meaningful and spiritually rewarding.

SET YOUR OBJECTIVE

Why are you fasting? Is it for spiritual renewal, for guidance, for healing, for the resolution of problems, for special grace to handle a difficult situation? Ask the Holy Spirit to clarify His leading and objectives for your prayer fast. This will enable you to pray more specifically and strategically.

MAKE YOUR COMMITMENT

Pray about the kind of fast you should undertake. Jesus implied that all of His followers should fast (Matthew 6:16–18; 9:14–15). For Him it was a matter of *when* believers would fast, not *if* they would do it.

PREPARE YOURSELF SPIRITUALLY

The very foundation of fasting and prayer is repentance. Unconfessed sin will hinder your prayers. Ask God to help you make a comprehensive list of your sins; then meditate on 1 John 1:9; Mark 11:25; Luke 11:4, 17:3–4. Make restitution as the Holy Spirit leads you, and ask God to fill you with His Holy Spirit according to His *command* in Ephesians 5:18 and His *promise* in 1 John 5:14–15. Finally, surrender your life fully to Jesus Christ as your Lord and Master; refuse to obey your worldly nature (Romans 12:1–2).

PREPARE YOURSELF PHYSICALLY

Fasting requires reasonable precautions. Consult your physician first, especially if you take prescription medication or have a chronic ailment. Some persons should never fast without professional supervision.

PUT YOURSELF ON A SCHEDULE

For maximum spiritual benefit, set aside ample time to be alone with the Lord. Listen for His leading. The more time you spend with Him, the more meaningful your fast will be.

When possible, begin and end each day on your knees with your spouse for a brief time of praise and thanksgiving to God. Longer periods of time with our Lord in prayer and study of His Word are often better spent alone.

END YOUR FAST GRADUALLY

Begin eating again gradually. Do not eat solid foods immediately after your fast. Suddenly reintroducing solid food to your stomach and digestive tract will likely have negative, even dangerous, consequences. Try several smaller meals or snacks each day. If you end your fast gradually, the beneficial physical and spiritual effects will result in continued good health.

EXPECT RESULTS

If you sincerely humble yourself before the Lord, repent, pray, and seek God's face; if you consistently meditate on His Word, you will experience a heightened awareness of His presence (John 14:21). The Lord will give you fresh, new spiritual insights. Your confidence and faith in God will be strengthened. You will feel mentally, spiritually, and physically refreshed. You will see answers to your prayers.

A single fast, however, is not a spiritual cure-all. Just as we need to be filled with the Holy Spirit daily, we also need new times of fasting before God. A twenty-four-hour fast each week has been greatly rewarding to many Christians.

It takes time to build your spiritual fasting muscles. If you fail to make it through your first fast, do not be discouraged. You may have tried to fast too long the first time out, or you may need to strengthen your understanding and resolve. As soon as possible, undertake another fast until you do succeed. God will honor you for your faithfulness.

Appendix F

God's Word on Active Prayer

Following are selected Scripture references that were presented throughout the text of this book. We encourage you to sit down with your Bible and review these verses in their context, prayerfully reflecting upon what God's Word tells you about the joy of active prayer.

CHAPTER 1

Hebrews 10:20

Hebrews 4:16

Psalm 145:18

CHAPTER 2

Romans 3:23

John 14:6

Acts 4:12

Romans 6:23

Revelation 1:6

2 Corinthians 12:10

1 Corinthians
1:27–29

Romans 8:11

1 Thessalonians 5:17

Luke 18:1

Proverbs 15:8

Jeremiah 33:3

CHAPTER 3

Matthew 6:6

Luke 11:1

James 5:16

Hebrews 10:19

Ephesians 2:18

Philippians 2:13

Romans 8:26

Romans 8:27

Ephesians 5:18–19

CHAPTER 4

Ephesians 6:18

Hebrews 12:28

Isaiah 57:15

1 John 3:21–22

John 4:23

Proverbs 21:1

CHAPTER 5

Psalm 66:18

Mark 11:25

Matthew 21:22

Matthew 9:29

John 15:7

James 4:2–3

John 14:14

John 16:24

Matthew 7:7–8

Matthew 17:20

James 1:6–8

Ephesians 2:8–9

Romans 10:17

Matthew 28:18–20

1 John 5:14–15

Hebrews 4:2

CHAPTER 6

John 14:12

Acts 4:24–30

CHAPTER 7

1 John 1:7–9

1 Thessalonians
  5:18

About the Author

DR. BILL BRIGHT, fueled by his passion to share the love and claims of Jesus Christ with "every living person on earth," was the founder and president of Campus Crusade for Christ. The world's largest Christian ministry, Campus Crusade serves people in 191 countries through a staff of 26,000 full-time employees and more than 225,000 trained volunteers working in some sixty targeted ministries and projects that range from military ministry to inner-city ministry.

Bill Bright was so motivated by what is known as the Great Commission, Christ's command to carry the gospel throughout the world, that in 1956 he wrote a booklet titled *The Four Spiritual Laws*, which has been printed in 200 languages and distributed to more than 2.5 billion people. Other books Bright authored include *Discover the Book God Wrote, God: Discover His Character, Come Help Change Our World, The Holy Spirit: The Key to Supernatural Living, Life Without Equal, Witnessing Without Fear, Coming Revival, Journey Home,* and *Red Sky in the Morning.*

In 1979 Bright commissioned the *JESUS* film, a feature-length dramatization of the life of Christ. To date, the film has been viewed by more than 5.7 billion people in 191 countries and has become the most widely viewed and translated film in history.

Dr. Bright died in July 2003 before the final editing of this book. But he prayed that it would leave a legacy of his love for Jesus and the power of the Holy Spirit to change lives. He is survived by his wife, Vonette; their sons and daughters-in-law; and four grandchildren.

THE LIFETIME TEACHINGS OF

Written by one of Christianity's most respected and beloved teachers, this series is a must for every believer's library. Each of the books in the series focuses on a vital aspect of a meaningful life of faith: trusting God, accepting Christ, living a spirit-filled life, intimacy with God, forgiveness, prayer, obedience, supernatural thinking, giving, and sharing Christ with others.

Dr. Bill Bright was the founder of Campus Crusade for Christ Intl., the world's largest Christian ministry. He commissioned the JESUS film, a documentary on the life of Christ that has been translated into more than 800 languages.

EACH BOOK INCLUDES A CELEBRITY-READ ABRIDGED AUDIO CD!

Joy of Trusting God
Foreword by Billy Graham
Audio by John Tesh
0-78144-246-X

Joy of Finding Jesus
Foreword by Pastor
Rick Warren
Audio by Naomi Judd
0-78144-247-8

Joy of Spirit-Filled Living
Foreword by Kay Arthur
Audio by Ricky Skaggs
0-78144-248-6

DR. BILL BRIGHT
FOUNDER OF CAMPUS CRUSADE FOR CHRIST

Joy of Supernatural Thinking
Foreword by John Maxwell
Audio by Gov. Mike Huckabee
0-78144-253-2

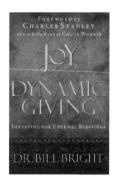

Joy of Dynamic Giving
Foreword by Charles Stanley
Audio by John Schneider
0-78144-254-0

Joy of Sharing Jesus
Foreword by Pat Robertson
Audio by Kathie Lee Gifford
0-78144-255-9

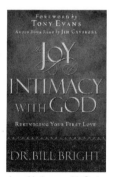

Joy of Intimacy with God
Foreword by Tony Evans
Audio by Amy Grant
0-78144-249-4

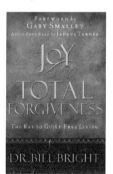

Joy of Total Forgiveness
Foreword by Gary Smalley
Audio by Janine Turner
0-78144-250-8

Joy of Active Prayer
Foreword by Max Lucado
Audio by Joni Earekcson Tada
0-78144-251-6

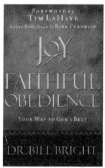

Joy of Faithful Obedience
Foreword by Tim LaHaye
Audio by Kirk Franklin
0-78144-252-4

Collect all 10 of These Foundational Works!

The Word at Work Around the World

A vital part of Cook Communications Ministries is our international outreach, Cook Communications Ministries International (CCMI). Your purchase of this book, and of other books and Christian-growth products from Cook, enables CCMI to provide Bibles and Christian literature to people in more than 150 languages in 65 countries.

Cook Communications Ministries is a not-for-profit, self-supporting organization. Revenues from sales of our books, Bible curricula, and other church and home products not only fund our U.S. ministry, but also fund our CCMI ministry around the world. One hundred percent of donations to CCMI go to our international literature programs.

CCMI reaches out internationally in three ways:

• Our premier International Christian Publishing Institute (ICPI) trains leaders from nationally led publishing houses around the world.

• We provide literature for pastors, evangelists, and Christian workers in their national language.

• We reach people at risk—refugees, AIDS victims, street children, and famine victims—with God's Word.

Word Power, God's Power

Faith Kidz, RiverOak, Honor, Life Journey, Victor, NexGen — every time you purchase a book produced by Cook Communications Ministries, you not only meet a vital personal need in your life or in the life of someone you love, but you're also a part of ministering to José in Colombia, Humberto in Chile, Gousa in India, or Lidiane in Brazil. You help make it possible for a pastor in China, a child in Peru, or a mother in West Africa to enjoy a life-changing book. And because you helped, children and adults around the world are learning God's Word and walking in his ways.

Thank you for your partnership in helping to disciple the world. May God bless you with the power of his Word in your life.

For more information about our international ministries, visit www.ccmi.org.

Additional copies of
THE JOY OF ACTIVE PRAYER
and other titles in "The Joy of Knowing God" series
are available wherever good books are sold.

✠ ✠ ✠

If you have enjoyed this book,
or if it has had an impact on your life,
we would like to hear from you.

Please contact us at:

VICTOR BOOKS
Cook Communications Ministries, Dept. 201
4050 Lee Vance View
Colorado Springs, CO 80918

Or at our Web site: www.cookministries.com

Victor®
The Bible Teacher's Teacher